MW01124991

How My *Divorce* Saved My *Marriage*

A Wife's Hard-Learned Tips, Strategies, and Advice to Prepare You for Marriage or to Heal and Restore the One You're Already In

April Moncrief

with Candice L Davis

How My Divorce Saved My Marriage

Copyright © 2015 by April Moncrief

All rights reserved. No part of this book may be reproduced or transmitted in any form or by any means without written permission of the author.

ISBN: 978-0-692-48044-1

To all women
fighting the
good fight for
your marriage:

Stay faithful.
Stay focused.
The best is
yet to come!

Contents

Why You Should Read This Book

Is marriage more work for you than *it should be?*

Do you ever feel like you're stuck in a mediocre relationship?
Ever think it might be easier to get a divorce?
Do you just want something . . . more?

By the time you could walk, our society had already started its campaign to convince you that you could have a perfect marriage someday. It didn't matter if your parents supported each other in every effort, or couldn't keep their hands off each other, or they suffered through a mediocre marriage, fought bitterly, or maybe never married at all.

Picture books, bedtime stories, TV shows, and movies promised you a great romance with your one true love, culminating with "I do." Every story ended with "happily ever after" and soul mates riding into the sunset. Cinderella got her prince, and so did Snow White and Belle and all the others. Lucky ladies.

You couldn't help taking in those idealized images, and even if you watched people in your family struggle through rough patches in their marriages, you were convinced your marriage would be different. You and your future husband—whatever tall, handsome, wealthy gentleman he might turn out to be—would never argue, and if you did quietly disagree on occasion, he'd bring home your favorite flowers and offer a sincere apology, and you'd make up with a passionate night of great sex. Either you'd both have high-powered jobs, making tons of money, or he'd be the perfect provider, so you could stay home, keep a perfect house, and cook gourmet meals, all while raising your 2.3 kids, each of whom would excel at sports and music and make straight As in school. Or you and your hubby would skip the kids and travel the world together.

The details of your dream marriage don't matter. What matters is that, when it comes to relationships, reality and fantasy rarely meet. If you're like most of us, you had no idea how hard marriage would be, how much the pressures and distractions of life would threaten your union, or how much heartache might taint the relationship that was supposed to fulfill you like nothing else ever would. Lucy and Ricky, Mr. and Mrs. Brady, Cliff and Clair Huxtable, and even Marge and Homer Simpson, all made it look, well, funny but easy.

I was convinced I'd have a *Cosby Show* kind of marriage, but I don't remember Clair ever packing up her kids and moving home with her parents like I did. I married my high school sweetheart, Herman, and we launched our careers with big ambitions, and had children. But soon after our twins reached one year of age, my husband and I had filed for divorce, and I was on my way back to Alabama to live with my mother until I could establish my new life as a single mom.

Thankfully, we weren't ready to give up on each other, even after all the drama and hurt. Don't get me wrong. We went through with the divorce. But we were lucky enough to share a moment when we were both ready to put pride aside, own our parts in the divorce, and fight to get our marriage back.

We quickly learned that we both had to change. The only way to restore our marriage and reunite our family was for each of us to work on ourselves first and for the two of us, as a couple, to agree to do whatever it took to create something better than what we had the first time around. We committed to changing as people and changing the way we interacted as a couple, and before the kids celebrated their third birthday, we'd put our family back together again.

We created something better than the image society sold us. And you can too.

Why I Wrote This Book

This book does not make me look good. In fact, when you read about the kind of wife I was in my first marriage, you're probably going to think I was a real bitch. And in a lot of ways, I was. So why would any woman air the dirty laundry of her marriage? Why would she put her own bad behavior on blast? Why would she pull back the curtain and let everyone see how she failed?

The answer is simple: I'm on a mission.

I'm on a mission to let other women know they're not the only ones who smile and laugh with their husbands in public and then go home and treat each other like crap. I'm on a mission to reassure other wives that they're not alone in struggling to figure out how to make a marriage work. I'm on a mission to help couples understand the true covenant of marriage and how it can make their lives easier, more enjoyable, and more fun.

After Herman and I remarried, I didn't expect the divorce to be a factor in our lives any more. We just wanted to love each other, raise our children and grow old together. End of story. I had no desire to wallow in the details of our story, and a lot of our friends and family didn't want to touch the subject of our divorce. In fact, many of them kind of pretended it hadn't happened. Who could blame them? Nobody wants to look at the dark side of another couple's marriage.

But other people watched us rebuilding our life together and wanted to know not only what happened to break us up but how we made it back. How could a marriage that always looked so strong from the outside have ended in a divorce? And how in the world did we fix things enough to get remarried?

Once I felt healed of my bad marriage and divorce wounds, I opened up to girlfriends and shared my experience. The more I engaged with people on the subject, the more they exposed their own marital problems. Mind you these were people I'd always thought had fabulous marriages. They kept up a good front because it was just too embarrassing to admit they couldn't figure out how to create what they pretended they already had.

The more honest I was about how my marriage fell apart, the more these people, mostly women, peeled back that pretty, shiny veneer covering the bad spots in their own relationships. Up until then, they'd felt like they had to put their heads down and live with their problems. As far as they could see, they only had two choices: be miserable or get divorced. They didn't realize they had a third option: to make the marriage better.

I couldn't give advice in the typical, guru-knows-all way, but I could share what I learned from my own my mistakes. I was shocked when friends came back and told me, "Girl, I tried that touch thing you talked about, and it worked." These people divulged their private business to me, listened to what I had to say, and put my advice into practice. I'd gone through all those challenges in our first marriage to find my purpose—to help women experience a true covenant of marriage, to help couples create something more than the transactional relationship marriage has become for so many people.

I'm a Christian, but I'm not about to tell you to just wait on Jesus, and let him make it right. I'm sharing practical steps you can take to enjoy a stronger, more secure, more fulfilling marriage. And you don't have to agree with my religious beliefs to benefit from my experience. Without question, I give God the glory for the restoration of my marriage, but what I learned in that process can be used by anyone.

My message is simple:

You can go through hell in your marriage, and still heal yourself and your relationship, sometimes even after the divorce papers have been signed. (And if you do all you can and find the marriage can't be healed, you can still heal yourself and move on.)

I wish I could say my husband and I have a perfect marriage now, that we agree on everything, and that there's no chance we'll ever grow apart again. But those would be straight up lies. There is no such thing as a perfect marriage. We still sometimes disagree and even argue, and I can't guarantee that we'll never find ourselves so far apart that we can't find our way back again. But we're doing pretty well now. We don't have to fake happiness anymore.

So I'm left with this mission. I never wanted to be the ambassador for divorce and remarriage, and that's not who I am. I'm an ambassador for conscious marriage, an advocate for doing the work so you can create something real and lasting, something better than any sitcom fantasy marriage.

How to Use This Book

It would be great if husband and wife both read this book at the same time. Even though I've written as if I'm speaking to the woman in the relationship, anyone can learn from the journey my husband and I went on to create a better marriage the second time around. If both parties in the marriage look at how they can apply the lessons that resonate, you may create a positive change in your marriage even faster.

That being said, ladies, don't try to force your husband to read this book if he's not interested. Focus on changing yourself rather than trying to change him. If he loves you and the relationship is important to him, there's a good chance he'll be inspired by the effort he sees you making and invest in making his own transformation.

Some of my opinions and some of the things I suggest you do will probably piss you off. That's good. It means I'm challenging you. You don't have to agree with me—especially not right away—but I ask that you hear me out.

Read with an open mind and the willingness to look in the mirror, recognize your own flaws, and make a change for the better. Don't try to read between the lines and look for what your husband should change. *Start with yourself.* I suggest reading this book from beginning to end. You may be surprised by things you can apply to your marriage.

If you're dealing with a specific issue in your marriage right now, and you feel an urgent need for help, flip to the lesson you think might be relevant. Consider how you can apply what you read to make your relationship better. Take action, and then go back and read the book from the beginning to understand the bigger picture.

The Love in Action tips sprinkled throughout are meant to give you practical, easy to implement steps you can take right now to strengthen your marriage and keep the love connection between you and your husband alive. They may seem one-sided; that's because they are. But most women will find that when they do some of these things for their husband, it won't take him long to return the favor.

If your marriage is pretty good, the lessons here will help you make it great. If your marriage is struggling, I hope you're able to use what I learned the hard way to get back on track. If you're seriously contemplating divorce, these lessons will help you make your decision with the utmost clarity and full awareness of what you're choosing. No matter what state your marriage is in right now, know that positive change is possible for you every day.

One Last, Very Important Thing

I do not advocate staying in an abusive marriage—whether that abuse is physical, verbal, mental, or emotional. Nothing in these pages can fix that level of dysfunction. If you're in an abusive relationship, put down this book and seek professional help in your area today.

The Rise and Fall of a Fairy Tale Marriage

Once upon a time, before I was a wife and mother, I was a wide-eyed teenage girl, a naive tomboy who loved playing sports and running around outside with the kids in my neighborhood. The summer of my sophomore year of high school, I met our high school's first black quarterback; of course he had graduated by this time. His family had just moved into our neighborhood, and his sister and I met and became close friends. His sister, a lot of her other friends, and I used to hang out at their house during the summer. Herman would walk into the room and say hello to everyone, but out of all of the girls in the crowded room, his eyes always seemed to stop on me. He would just stare and smile at me and then go on about his business. He did this every time I was hanging out at their house.

Herman Moncrief, the star quarterback, went from dating cheerleaders and "popular" girls to pursuing this scrawny, timid tenth-grader. We shared my first real kiss, but when he left for college, I assumed he'd be surrounded by all those college women and quickly forget about me.

When the first letter from my summer crush arrived, I melted. I couldn't believe it. In my mind, he was my boyfriend from that moment on. My mother didn't want me talking to boys yet—she didn't want me ending up a teen mom like so many girls in our town—but I was so flattered. All my life, my family had pumped me up to believe I was the prettiest and smartest girl in any room, and Herman's attention confirmed all that. I spent that whole next school year scribbling his name all over my notebooks and folders.

He wrote me every week, and I waited by the mailbox for his letters. For some reason, we opened up to each other. He didn't have to put on a front for me, and I could be real with him. Maybe it was easier to be honest when we were building our relationship in writing. Whatever the reason, we talked about the struggles our families had gone through and shared our dreams for the future, trusting each other with our most intimate thoughts.

Later he would tell me, "When I first saw you, all I wanted to do was take care of you." He did take care of me, and I happily let him. As the youngest of fifteen children, I was already spoiled, so it was easy to let him do things for me. Even though I worked, he gave me money and he also let me use his credit cards. He was a natural provider, and not just for me. He helped out any of his family whenever they needed it.

Where I'm from, it wasn't uncommon for people to either drop out of high school or, after graduation, go to work for one of the local factories in our hometown. Maybe they had to work to take care of their families, or maybe they just didn't think they were college material. Looking around me, I realized I didn't want to do either of those things.

I started hanging with my friends who were kind of from the other side of the tracks. These girls constantly talked about going to college, and they were preparing themselves for the process by getting good grades, studying for admissions tests, and joining the right organizations. I woke up to the fact that I needed to be doing the same things.

I obsessed so much over having more than a simple country life that people around me started calling me snooty. It didn't matter. I wanted higher education and a career, and when it was my turn to apply to college, Herman helped me figure out the financial aid process. Then he transferred to the same college I decided to attend.

Ten years after we started dating, the love of my life and I threw a big wedding and became husband and wife. We built great careers and bought a nice home in the suburbs of Atlanta. Everything seemed perfect—except when I didn't get what I wanted, and what I wanted most, at that point in our lives, was a baby. Even though I always saw myself in a high-powered, professional position, I also dreamed of having two kids, a dog, and a white picket fence. As soon as I saw thirty on the horizon, it seemed like all of our friends were having babies, and I stopped caring that the other parts of our plan hadn't come together yet.

I pushed, and he withdrew. I insisted, and we argued. I kept at him, and he finally relented. I didn't see the hairline fractures appearing in our marriage until it was too late.

I got the positive pregnancy test, and he was just as happy as I was. During my pregnancy, he took great care of me. And then one day, I went for an unscheduled prenatal appointment because I was sicker than my friends and family thought I should be, and the doctor uttered those four words that changed our lives forever, "I see two heartbeats." That was all he said. But in my mind, I heard, "Two separate heartbeats? Twins? Not one, but two mouths to feed?"

I called Herman at work to tell him the good news, and he responded with silence. What I didn't realize was that I'd just doubled the pressure on him to make sure he did everything possible to provide for his family. Those fractures in our relationship widened into deep cracks.

We loved our twins, Bryce and Asia, even before they came into the world. But once they were born, Herman and I were no longer husband and wife. We were just Momma and Daddy, each of us working full-time jobs, taking care of the babies in different ways, and forgetting all about taking care of each other.

Within a year, we had signed divorce papers.

So much for the image I crafted over the years of our perfect marriage. Initially, I tried to buy a house nearby so he could see the kids regularly, and honestly, so I could stay near him and hold out hope for us getting back together. Once I realized that wasn't going to happen, I decided to move back home to Alabama, leaving him in Georgia. He didn't realize what he'd lost until the moving truck pulled out of the driveway and what used to be our lively home became a constant reminder of the life and family he used to have.

Almost every weekend, Herman visited the twins, and it didn't take long for us to realize we still wanted to be together. We started dating again, with a hope for reconciliation, and with counseling from a pastor who really understood how to make a modern marriage work, we slowly came back together. With a lot of prayer and a sincere willingness to change ourselves for the sake of our relationship, we were one of the lucky couples able to put our family back together again.

But the work continues.

Where did you get your idea of what marriage should look like?

Does your vision of marriage make sense for you and your husband?

Are you fighting to force your relationship to reflect a vision that wasn't meant for you?

Write the right vision and make it plain.

The year I turned nine years old, a television show that would have a major impact on much of American culture hit the airwaves. A two-parent, highly educated, professional, upper-middle-class, African American family came into our homes every Thursday night. It showed me things I'd never seen for myself. For me, it opened up a whole new world of possibilities. I was hooked and spent the next several years watching *The Cosby Show*, and later the spin-off, *A Different World*, and imagining that TV life was mine.

All of the kids in my neighborhood would all be outside playing, and just before seven o'clock, someone would yell, "The Cosby Show's coming on!" In minutes, the streets would be empty. While my mother cooked dinner, my siblings and I piled into the den. I can still feel myself sliding across the wood floor to get to my place in front of the television. If we wanted to talk or get up and go to the bathroom, we waited for the commercial break.

Even at such a young age, I related to Clare Huxtable, the mother of five, and wanted everything she had. Here was a professional woman who looked like me, had a beautiful home, loved and honored the husband who loved and honored her, kept her mischievous but well-behaved children in check, and ran her house like a tight, love-filled ship. She was no joke, and everybody around her knew it. I wanted that power, that respect, and that acknowledgment. I wanted to be Clare Huxtable. Nobody wanted to miss a punchline.

After high school, I went to a historically black university, just like the young people on *A Different World* did, but I still had Clare in my sights. I planned to go to law school and become a suit-wearing attorney like her. And when Herman and I talked about our future, I set about designing our union (in my own mind) to look like Mr. and Mrs. Huxtable's marriage.

Only in stillness can you separate all that noise from what's true. I was never in to writing down my goals the way my husband has always done, but honestly, my vision for our marriage was so clear in my mind, I didn't think I needed to put it on paper. We were going to be the power couple, and I would do anything I had to do to make it happen. I included Herman in my plans, of course, and we had long conversations about what we

> *Tonight, let him come home and wind down with no responsibilities. Leave his dinner warming, fire up his favorite show, and let him have a couple of hours to himself.*

wanted our life together to look like. But what did we know? We were still kids.

By the time we made it official, we weren't children anymore, but we still didn't know much about this grown folks' business called marriage. We had this fanciful idea of what we wanted, but truthfully, not a clue what we'd gotten ourselves into. As we got deeper into married life, and things weren't going the way I wanted, I dug in and worked harder to get what I thought I wanted. The more I fought for it, the farther away this dream life I had in my head seemed to be.

After the divorce, I realized I'd been so lost in my own image of what our family should look like, act like, and do, that I never thought to consult God about how we should create the kind of relationship that was best for us. I let a TV show dictate to me how I should live my life. It was such a present influence, it felt real to me, but believe me when I say it was nothing like my reality. I'd struggled to attain the unattainable, and like a TV show with a bad script, our marriage had ended up canceled.

One of the biggest decisions we've made since we remarried was the choice to relocate to a new state so Herman could take a position that fast-tracked his career. While I had encouraged him to pursue the position, I didn't think he'd really want to take it—until the day he came home and said he had an offer. I had no intention of relocating to Nashville from Atlanta, but I could see how important the potential for advancement was to him. By then, he was the sole provider for our family, and he took that responsibility incredibly seriously. How could I backpedal when it clearly meant so much to him?

I felt lost and scared. I didn't want to leave behind the community we'd created for ourselves—our friends, our church, my moms' group, the children's school—and I didn't want to let my husband down. We had a lot of intense conversations, and I spent a lot of nights crying to myself. None of this fit with the vision I had for our second-time-around marriage.

Finally, I realized what I was missing. I was leaving God out of the equation. I needed to ask what his vision was for us, and then I needed to step back and listen. His was the vision I needed to write and make plain, not the one I'd invented.

So often in the Christian community, we like to quote Habakkuk 2:2. "Write the vision and make it plain," we say, and then we run off talking about how we're going to tell God what we want and be plain about it. But I recently discovered that when we take that verse out of context, we're missing the whole point of it. In chapter one of Habakkuk, the author talks to God. In chapter two, he's *listening* to God and taking down God's vision. *"The LORD gave me this answer: 'Write down clearly on tablets what I reveal to you, so that it can be read at a glance.'"* (Habakkuk 2:2 TEV)

I'm no Biblical scholar, but I can read. That book provides a clear example of talking first and then being receptive to answers. I'd been trying to force my vision on things and all along God was redirecting me to what he held in store for us. I needed to open myself up to his vision.

We're told to write down God's vision, but we've watered down the idea to the simplicity of a vision board. We've interpreted it to mean that all we have to do is be clear with God about what we want. Whether you live at the church or put your faith in the Universe, getting quiet is key to knowing what the right vision is for your life and for your marriage.

The problem with creating your vision out of whole cloth is that you've been under influences from television, movies, love songs, and other fairy tales for all your life. Your own family may have left you with an image you're running from or running toward for your marriage, but that doesn't mean it's the right one for you.

Start by meditating on, praying about, or journaling what you really want from your marriage. Do you want to feel safe and secure, have lots of excitement, or provide consistency for each other? Do you want peace and calm or great adventure? Focus on the end states you want to achieve. Then sit quietly and listen. Record in your journal what you'll have to do on a daily basis to achieve those ends.

Only in stillness can you separate yourself from the noise of all the images of a "perfect marriage" the world's tried to feed you. Be patient, expect an answer, and listen for it. Then you can write the right vision, make it plain, and go on to manifest it.

Light scented candles around the house and turn down most of the lights. Do a quick clean and welcome him home to a tidy, sweet-smelling escape from his day.

Is there someone in your husband's life you can't even pretend to like?

Does he have a close friend or sibling you just can't seem to click with?

Do you ever fantasize about the marriage you could have if your mother-in-law, sister-in-law, or _____ didn't come between you?

Open your heart to the people he loves.

I was born and raised in a small town in the South. One thing country people learn from birth is the importance of respecting your elders, but as a teenager, I came up against a woman who could make me forget all about manners and respect. I didn't know it at the time, but she would one day be my mother-in-law.

Herman, the popular, handsome quarterback, dated lots of girls before I came along. When I entered the picture, his mother must've seen something different in the way he was with me, and whatever it was, she didn't like it. It seemed as if she disliked me almost from the moment we met, and my response was to defend myself against what I saw as her unfair attacks. Looking back, I see a mother wanting to keep her youngest son close to her, but at the time, I only knew she and I were like fire and gasoline. Put us together, and something was bound to explode.

When Herman and I first started dating, I was still in high school, and he was working a full-time job and preparing to go off to college. This was well before cell phones put text-messaging, emails, and constant phone calls at everybody's fingertips. Instead, we passed notes—yes, folded pieces of paper—back and forth. We were crazy in love, the way only teenagers can be, so we wanted to be in touch with each other all the time. Since his younger sister went to school with me, she became our messenger.

After school one day, I called Herman and asked if he'd gotten a note I sent him. When he asked his sister about it, she denied ever getting a note from me. The conversation quickly became a disagreement, and it escalated to an argument. Over the phone, I could hear the two of them going at it in the typical big brother and little sister kind of way.

While he's in the shower, throw a big towel in the dryer for just a few minutes. Surprise him with the warm fluffy towel.

Then the family drama went to the next level. She started yelling and Herman lost his temper. Realizing how mad he really was, she locked herself in the bathroom, but he was too angry to let it end there. He went to the kitchen and got a knife to force the lock. Meanwhile, I got tired of waiting for him to come back to the phone, so I hung up and went outside to hang with my friends without thinking anything else of it. As the youngest of fifteen children, I'm well aware that siblings fight. No big deal, in my house anyway.

The next day at school, Herman's younger sister approached me to ask what I'd told him.

"All I did was ask him if he got my letter," I told her.

She went on to explain that when their mom came home from work that evening, she saw how angry Herman was with her and threatened to put him out of her house. Somehow, his picking the lock had become a story about him chasing his sister with a knife. And it was all my fault. That's right. Little ole' me had instigated a huge fallout between him and his sister.

After that, I got a cold reception from his mother when I showed up at their house. Either she wouldn't respond when I spoke to her, or she'd tell me, "Don't come up in my house starting nothing." If Herman got angry about the way she treated me, it just made her dislike me more for causing him to lose his temper. I tried to stay in my place, but I've never been the kind of person to just let anybody say whatever they want to me and not say anything back. I'd stand flat-footed across the room and give back what she was giving me, and when I was finished, I'd slam the door on the way out.

These days, we can all tell the story of how Herman was ready to kill his little sister over me and laugh about it, but for almost twenty years none of it was very funny. There was rarely a time my mother-in-law and I were together that didn't end in an argument. The constant tension meant Herman could never feel comfortable leaving his wife and his mother alone in a room together. Whenever we had a conflict, I wanted my husband to rush to my defense and take my side, but instead he'd tell me to ignore it. It just wasn't enough for me, and that ongoing rivalry was one of the contributing factors that led to our divorce. I wanted him to put me first, but he was torn between his wife and his mother.

Later, we met with a counselor who told Herman to remember that as his wife, I was his first ministry, and that while he should never disrespect his mother, he couldn't allow anyone—not even her—to disrespect his wife. He took the advice to heart. When things became heated between his mother and me, he started hesitantly taking my side and telling her it wasn't the time or place. He put himself between us as a wall of protection, and as I saw him stand up for me, I realized I needed to do my part. This man was under way too much stress trying to mediate between the two women he loved, and I had to find a way to make it easier on him.

I looked for ways to connect with my mother-in-law. I started to see her with fresh eyes, and I saw things about her that I could empathize with and respect. As I responded to her with more calm and kindness, my marriage with her son reached a new level of maturity. He so clearly appreciated the effort I was making, it only made me want to do more and be better. His sanity, his peace, and his blood pressure were more important to me than winning an argument with her.

My relationship with my mother-in-law has grown by leaps and bounds. We now have a mutual respect for one another, and we have finally become good friends. I love and respect her like my own mom.

If you're struggling to get along with someone your husband loves, and that tension is damaging your marriage, open up to him and tell him what you really need. Don't demand that he confront that person or sever ties, but let him know how important it is for you to feel like no other relationship comes before his marriage. Allow him to handle it in his own way, and show your appreciation for his effort when he does. While you don't need to tolerate blatant mistreatment, learn to put your own need to be right aside and allow that person's comments and opinions to wash over you. For your husband's sake, try to find areas of common interest that you and this person can talk about and bond over without winding up in conflict with each other.

> Surprise him with a weekend off from his "Honey Do" list. Let him sleep in and wake up to a quiet house, a nice breakfast, and nothing to do.

Most importantly, take care of yourself and your marriage. When you're confident in who you are as a woman and as a wife, when you know your marriage is solid and your husband loves you, you'll find it a lot easier to accept and open your heart to the people he loves.

Do the Joneses annoy you because they have an affectionate, conflict-free, apparently anointed marriage?

Are you trying to control everything in your house so your marriage and family life fit your image of perfection?

Are you disappointed, stressed out, and angry because your marriage is fast becoming the kind of relationship you said you'd never have?

Stop trying to have (or look like you have) the perfect marriage.

I t was the best day of my life, like a fantasy come true. I'd pulled off the extravagant wedding ceremony I dreamed of having. I was enjoying our reception, until a friend leaned over and told me, "They're saying he's working all the time, and you're spending all his money on this wedding." She pointed out a couple of people sitting across the room.

"Well, I have a job too," I thought. "Some of my money paid for this." After all, I was the one who made the payments on my wedding dress. Buying over time was the only way I could afford the over-the-top, $1000 gown and veil I found at a high-priced boutique. Herman tried to reign in my spending, so I compromised by agreeing to artificial flowers, as opposed to the beautiful, very expensive, live flowers I initially wanted. But I wasn't willing to sacrifice my dress. Instead, I spent "my" money on it.

And while I was spending, I encouraged my friends to invest in my vision as well. For some odd reason, a few of my fifteen bridesmaids thought the $300 I wanted them to spend on their dresses was too much money. A couple of them said they couldn't afford to be in the wedding, and they dropped out of the wedding party. I eventually gave in and switched to a less expensive bridesmaid's dress, but back to my own money, I spent over $1000 on the wedding photos, including a pre-wedding shoot for a portrait of the beautiful bride in her wedding gown to display at the reception. I also paid someone to make a video that would showcase photos of us, and I brought in praise dancers to perform.

Whatever other people thought, I wanted a lavish, memorable event, and I wanted to be the center of attention for that one special day. I wanted glamour! After ten years together, I thought we deserved a fabulous event to celebrate our love. We were baked and simmered in that relationship, fortified and ready for the long haul. I wanted our wedding to reflect all that and more.

Text him to say "I love you" when he least expects it so he knows you think of him when you're apart.

Looking back, we actually had an overblown version of a little country wedding. We got married in our hometown with all of our family and friends who had seen our relationship grow since high school, so I had to do something grand. In my mind, we were the couple people expected to do big things, and that included our wedding. More importantly, I expected us to do things bigger and better than anyone else.

For our honeymoon, we flew off to spend a week in Jamaica, but on the fourth day, I told Herman I was ready to go home early. I told him I was bored, but what I really wanted to do was get back to my friends, gloat over our wedding photos, and talk about how wonderful everything had been. I wanted to bask in our recent nuptials a little bit. It didn't occur to me how incredibly ungrateful it was to suggest that we cut our trip short when my husband had worked so hard to pay for it.

Herman blew up, and we had the first argument of our marriage. Later that night, he shared with me that while I'd been throwing cash at the wedding, he'd been dealing with the news that the company he worked for was shutting down. The accounting firm he was employed with at the time was connected to a multi-national utility company accused of stealing billions of dollars from their employees and clients. Just like that company, the accounting firm would be closing its doors in the wake of one of the biggest corporate scandals of the decade. He'd been under tremendous pressure for weeks, and I'd been so caught up in planning our extravaganza that I hadn't even noticed.

While part of me thought he should've told me what was going on, regardless of the fact that all employees had been ordered to keep it quiet, a bigger part of me felt like a spoiled brat, the kind of bride you expect to see screaming at the caterer or throwing a drink in her maid of honor's face on a reality TV show. Throughout the wedding planning process, our world revolved around me and what I wanted.

Sometimes it can look like a big wedding is all about the image the couple projects to the world, but that wasn't really the issue for me. Yes, I enjoyed the spectacle of having an elaborate, expensive wedding. We were the "it" couple—Herman, the star football player, who went off to college with the potential to do big things, and April, a small town girl with big dreams. Everybody knew settling down in a trailer on a small plot of land and popping out a couple of kids wasn't the goal for me. I wanted more than a small town life.

Sure, I hoped people would see our wedding as special, but more than that, I envisioned our perfect wedding as the beginning of the perfect marriage I expected us to have. It wasn't just about impressing folks. I was convinced that even though we didn't have many real examples of a happy, successful marriage, we were so much the exception to the rule we could surpass success and get to perfection.

We knew what not to do. We swore we wouldn't be like our parents when it came to marriage. We intended to do whatever we could to overcome the dysfunction we witnessed as children. I'd spent all those years planning and dreaming about having a perfect relationship with my future husband. Those plans became expectations for me, and I thought they would protect us from failing in our marriage.

I would land a prestigious job with a great salary and eventually go to law school. Herman would continue to grow and advance in his career, climbing the executive ranks. We'd buy our dream home and have children before I turned thirty. I'd mapped it all out, but as time passed and those things didn't come to fruition on schedule, I became resentful. I became a control freak, trying to make things happen the way I'd expected. My desire to do and have those things in my own time led to many of the arguments that destroyed our relationship. I tried to control my way to a perfect marriage. Instead, we got divorced.

We had a fancier wedding than our parents and most of our relatives. We put on the show of being an ambitious, in love, up-and-coming power couple, and in a lot of ways, that's what we were. But we still wound up signing divorce papers.

Our second wedding couldn't have been more different from the first, in all the most wonderful ways. We remarried on what would've been our original anniversary date. Herman and I gathered at the church with less than twenty people, just our parents and a couple of friends, the preacher, and a photographer. No pomp, no circumstance. Our family of four all wore blue jeans and white button-down shirts.

Herman and I both felt the deep seriousness of our decision to try again, so much so that we were actually nervous. This time, we knew it wouldn't be easy and we'd have to work for the kind of relationship we wanted. In the calm and quiet of the nearly empty church, we felt the presence of the Lord as we prepared to make a new commitment with God at the center. The perfect marriage may not exist, but I have to confess that second wedding was absolute perfection for us.

After the ceremony, Bryce and Asia went home with their grandparents. My new husband and I spent our wedding night at the same hotel where we stayed on our first wedding night, but the new Mr. and Mrs. Moncrief differed greatly from the overly confident young couple we once were. On that second wedding night, we felt anxious about the roles we were stepping into. The ceremony was nice, but this time, we were hyper-aware that it was only the beginning.

There's nothing inherently wrong with throwing a big wedding to celebrate your love or just because you like a good party. As long as you both want it and can afford it, you have every right to the ceremony and reception that make you happy and reflect your values. But in my case, that first wedding was the beginning of trying to do the impossible task of creating perfection.

You and your husband are flawed people, just like my husband and I and everyone else on this planet. Expecting two fallible beings to come together and manifest perfection defies common sense. There's a reason why those vows include "for better and for worse." The worse will come. You will have struggles in your marriage. Expect them. Prepare for them, and do your best to allow them to draw you closer together.

Plan a date night outside of the house and away from family stresses and responsibilities. Spend a few hours being his girlfriend again.

Don't spend too much time focusing on the things you don't want in your marriage. If you do, you'll likely create what you're running from because you're giving your attention to the wrong things. Instead, think about how you can build a loving, solid marriage on a daily basis.

Set goals and work toward them, but worry less about ticking off accomplishments on your checklist and more about how you'll make big decisions together, handle disagreements, and make each other feel cared for and loved.

Pray about the things you want in your marriage, but know that God's timing, may not be your timing and accept that you can't do the impossible. You can have a good, even great marriage, but it can never be perfect. Recognizing that will free you to build the best marriage you and your husband can have together.

Are you constantly tired and irritated because it seems no one in your house will help you with all that needs to be done?

Do you feel like you have to do it all—earn as much money as you can, keep a perfect house, and help your husband chop brush, carry wood, and dig holes for the new fence?

Are you convinced your home will fall apart if you don't have a hand in everything?

Embrace your role as wife.

While Herman held up one end, I hefted my end of the sofa and started up the two flights of stairs. We were moving into our first place together. As we maneuvered our way along, one of our new neighbors came out of his apartment and saw what we were doing. "You need help?" he asked.

"No, thanks," Herman told him. "She's got it."

The neighbor looked at me and shook his head. "Girl, you don't need to do that," he said, and he came over to lend a hand.

That little moment planted a seed in me. Maybe, just maybe, Herman and I had different roles to play. Maybe I didn't have to do everything he did. It would take years for me to really get it, but that was the first time it even occurred to me that the differences between men and women might lead us to take on distinct responsibilities. Obviously, I knew he was physically stronger than I was, but that didn't stop me from trying to match him step for step in moving furniture, mowing the grass, and landscaping the yard. I'd watched my mother do it all as I was growing up, and I became convinced that was just the role of a wife.

You can do it all. Anything he can do, you can do better. Be his better half. Be his helpmate.

Those messages came at me from all sides, and I interpreted them to mean I had to try to be my husband's equal in all things. We even had a running line about it when we got married the first time. "Everybody who eats and drinks in here is going to work," we'd say. The problem was that all the things I did to maintain our home fell outside of the category of work. We didn't really consider all the shopping and cleaning and scheduling and running around as my contribution to our household. It was just what I was supposed to do.

I would take care of the inside of our house, and then I'd help Herman cut the grass, pull weeds, and clear out the brush. If it needed to be done, my job, I thought, was to jump right in there next to my husband and do it—all this in addition to working non-stop to maintain an immaculate home for us and holding down my full-time job. Once the twins were born, I took on most of the chores that came with raising two infants as well.

While I truly believed I was doing the right thing for our family, taking on so much left me bitter, tired, and irritable. In my constant state of exhaustion, it didn't take much to set me off, and neither Herman nor I fully understood most of that stemmed from me overextending myself. I wanted him to help me more, so I nagged and begged and fussed. I didn't grasp that the problem was almost entirely within my control. It wasn't just that he needed to do more. *I also needed to do less.*

After the divorce, one of the most helpful counselors we saw was a pastor in our hometown of Prattville, Alabama. He gave us a word of advice that would make all the difference to us in our second marriage. "Let him be the husband," he told me. "God created him specifically for this reason, to take care of you and his family." And he admonished Herman, "Allow her to be your wife. She is a special creature, a gift from God. Treat her as such."

For whatever reason, we'd both reached a place where we could receive such a simple, yet powerful message. Herman started treating me with kid gloves, constantly checking on my wellbeing, handling me like I was precious to him. I began to take some things off my own to-do list. Maybe he would pick them up. Maybe they wouldn't get done. But I was finished trying to be his equal and more. I was over trying to do everything he did on top of everything I had to do.

After we remarried and the twins and I moved back to Atlanta, I settled in and told Herman I'd try to see if I could get my old job back. When he suggested I should wait for a while, it caught me off guard. Eventually, we both decided that with all the demands of taking care of Bryce and Asia, it didn't make sense for me to rush off to work. It turned out that our family functioned much better with me at home, running the household, and Herman bringing in the income.

That's not the case for every family. Many women prefer to go to work full-time, and even more have no choice. They have to work to keep the lights on and the hot water running. But embracing your role as his wife isn't about whether you work outside of the home or not.

The role of the wife is to support, uplift, and encourage your husband. Of course, you have to take on part of the workload, whether it be inside of the home, outside of the home, or both. But too many of you are trying to match your husband's time at the office hour for hour, run the kids to swim and soccer, come home and make dinner, plant flowers around the mailbox, and make sure the house is dust-free from top to bottom. Then you get angry with your husband because he's not doing enough.

Maybe he's not.

But the real problem is that you, the wife, are doing too much.

Maybe you're thinking, "Well, if I don't do it, it won't get done." How do you know? Perhaps your husband will pick up some of the slack. Even small kids can pitch in, and there are some jobs you can hire a professional to do. Yes, sometimes there will be things that don't get done or don't get done to your usual standard, but you have to learn to be all right with that. It's better than running yourself into the ground because you think that's what it means to be a good wife.

Embracing your role as his wife means loving, supporting, and encouraging your husband, but it also means setting some limits. If you're a woman of faith, you know God designed you to be your husband's blessing. You are not the husband, therefore you shouldn't hold yourself responsible for doing everything he does.

If you're overwhelmed, talk to your husband about how you can have a more equitable division of labor in your family. If you both work outside of the home, then you, as the wife, can't possibly be expected to take on all that goes into running the house as well. If one of you cooks dinner every day, perhaps the other one can be responsible for cleaning the kitchen. If you're driving the children to all of their activities, maybe your husband takes full responsibility for the yard, or perhaps the two of you can make room in your budget to pay a service or a teenager in your neighborhood to cut the grass and plant the tulips.

Send a sexy text to let him know you can't wait for him to get home. And tell him how you'll be waiting for him... in bed.

You cannot do it all. The sooner you accept that, the better off you'll be.

The idea that you can bring home the bacon, fry it up in a pan, and look sexy doing it all might make for entertaining TV commercials, but in real life, it makes for a lot of unhappy women and miserable marriages. Do yourself and your husband a favor, let him be the husband, while you focus on your role as his wife.

Is there something you've been trying to tell your husband that he can't seem to hear?

Do you really want to hear your husband's thoughts and opinions?

Do you feel alone, like you've got no one to talk to? Does he?

Practice effective communication.

A few months after the twins were born, I stood in the driveway, waved goodbye to my sisters, and watched them drive off. They were headed to Alabama to visit with the rest of our family before returning to Connecticut, where they lived at the time. One of my sisters had come to stay with us for a few months right before the twins were born, but it was time for her to go home, and another sister came down to get her. We spent the day hanging out, laughing, and enjoying each other's company, but now, for the first time, it was just me and my infant twins.

I went inside, and laid the babies on a blanket on the floor. Then I lay down beside them and bawled my head off. There we were, the three of us just crying our eyes out together. We must've been a pitiful sight.

I don't know why the babies were crying in that moment, but I was crying because I still needed help, and it seemed no one really understood what I was taking on. My sister, who'd been with me from the last half of my pregnancy through the first weeks of the babies lives, had just left me. My closest family was two hours away, and I didn't think I could impose on my friends by asking them to give me a hand. My husband was working long hours, and our relationship wasn't in a good place. Besides, he wasn't any more mentally prepared to care for Bryce and Asia than I was.

All of the crying and feeling overwhelmed and needing to get away from the kids, did I experience a little postpartum depression? I'd say it was more like the baby blues, aggravated by feeling isolated. Staying home all day when I was accustomed to going to work, taking primary responsibility for two screaming babies, keeping our home clean and orderly, living hours away

> Remember when you were dating and you couldn't go five steps without holding his hand? Take your marriage back to romance by walking hand-in-hand again.

from my mom and sisters and never having a moment to myself all dragged me down to a sad, dark place. Although I knew my sister had to leave eventually, and that I had to figure out how to take care of the kids myself, in the wake of her departure I felt lonely before she even hit the highway. Feeling like I had nobody to talk to about it and that my partner for life couldn't hear what I needed him to hear only made it worse.

It didn't occur to me that my husband was going through his own difficult transition to parenthood, and that he wasn't being heard either. For whatever reasons, he couldn't share his experience with me. He retreated into silence, and I resorted to screaming and making demands. Both of those strategies worked about as well as you'd expect them to work.

Our family underwent two incredibly stressful life changes, the birth of the babies and Herman's new job, within a very short period of time, and we couldn't figure out how to share our emotions or problem-solve together. Like many couples, we hadn't taken the time to learn how to communicate effectively. The more stress our marriage came under, the more we paid the price for our inability to openly share our fears, worries, and needs.

It's never too late to learn how to talk to each other, but unfortunately, we didn't figure that part out until after we were divorced. And we're still working on it and getting better at it every day.

While I was in the middle of writing this book, Herman received a job offer in another city—another state, no less. I had encouraged him to apply for the position, but when it became a real possibility, I wasn't sure I wanted to uproot our family and move hours away from the friends we'd made over the last several years.

This time we talked through all of the pros and cons a new job could bring with it. My husband tried to paint the most honest picture he could of how our lives would change, and the bottom line was that I should expect to be running the house and taking care of the kids by myself again. The job would consume all of his time and energy for the first few years, and I could either accept that or he could turn the job down.

Neither of us was willing to risk our family again, but the kids were older and more self-sufficient, the opportunity was tempting, and I had a much better handle on how to run the house more or less on my own. In the end, I was cool with the decision to move, but you'd better believe we spent hours and hours discussing all the possible problems and solutions and making sure we ended up on the same page.

To get to that place of agreement, we used the communication skills we'd learned through the counseling leading up to our second marriage. Here are some of the most important tools we use. Put them to practice and add whatever you need as a couple. Of course, all of this works better when both of you are willing to put in the effort, but you have to be responsible for your side of any conversation.

Tools for Effective Communication

Listen. This is the most important tool in your communication toolbox. It's also the hardest one to use when you need it the most. In the middle of an argument, the last thing you want to do is listen. But you must. I know it feels like what you have to say is more important, but it's just not true.

Don't interrupt him while he's speaking. It's so disrespectful to try to shout him down because you don't like where he's going with his point. Trust me. Things go a lot better when you wait for your turn to speak. And please don't sit there pretending to listen while you're formulating your next comeback. You love this man, so you should care about his thoughts and opinions. When you both take time to really listen to each other, you can prevent a disagreement from escalating to a fight.

Put aside your unrealistic expectations. Don't expect him to think like you think, accept what you say as the only way, or give you everything you want. You wouldn't expect anyone else in the world to jump on board just because you said so, and it's unreasonable to think your husband will either.

Get humble. Be prepared to recognize and acknowledge when he's right or has a good point. Nobody's right all the time, so open your mind to the possibility that you're occasionally wrong. Give his position serious consideration, and give him credit when it's due. After all, would you really have married someone who couldn't confidently come up with a good idea every once in a while.

Empathize. He might act like he doesn't, but he has feelings just like you and I do. Put yourself in his shoes to understand what might be making him angry or distant when you disagree.

Talk about the bad *and* the good. Sometimes we get so focused on discussing problems, we forget to share good news and funny moments, and compliments and appreciation fall by the wayside. Other times, we sweep problems under the rug and act like everything is okay when serious issues need to be addressed. Find a balance between addressing the negative and celebrating the positive.

Agree to discuss tough issues when both parties are ready to talk. Even though you want to have a discussion right this minute, you can't assume he's ready to engage in what might be a difficult conversation. When you force him to talk about an issue before he's prepared to do so, you're much more likely to have an argument. Instead, ask him to give you a time when he'd prefer to come together to chat and then give him some space.

Don't over-share. Most men like to get to the point, and they're a lot more willing to talk when they know you can do the same. Maybe you want to share the whole story and every detail of your thought process, so he can really understand your position. Maybe you think he just needs more information, so he can understand how right you are. From the point of view of the person listening to you, a five-minute monologue can be over-whelming. Sometimes less is more.

Stay away from those hot-button issues. If your husband has been out of work for six months, a discussion about whose turn it is to do the dishes probably isn't the right time to bring up his lengthy unemployment. You've got to play fair, ladies. That's your husband. Think about that for a minute. That's the man you committed your life to loving and supporting. Stop reaching deep into your arsenal to find the sharpest weapon you can use to cut him just so you can win an argument.

Be flexible. Maybe you two had an agreement on the issue in the past. Maybe you had a specific plan in place. Things change. Be willing to come back to the table and start the discussion again.

Be prepared to apologize. Sometimes all it takes is a sincere "I'm sorry" to cool down a volatile situation. If both of you let your egos get in the way, that apology may never come. Why drag things on unnecessarily? Be willing to apologize, especially when you know you've played some part in things going off track.

Use the gift of touch. Reaching out to put your hand on your husband can change the tenor of the whole conversation, especially when you have positive, caring intentions behind it.

Ask him about his work day, and really listen. Save the stresses of your own day for a later conversation.

Know when to let it go. It gets easier with practice, but no matter how hard you try to be a great communicator, things still go bad sometimes. You know yourself well enough to recognize when you're ready to fight, and you should pay attention to the signs that your husband is getting heated. If you feel your conversation turning into something ugly, walk away. Pick up the subject again when you're both calm.

You know that perfect couple that never argues and only speaks to each other in the most loving way? Yeah, that's the side you see in public. Any two people who've intertwined their lives and who have to make decisions that affect both of them in equal measure will sometimes have conflict. No matter how good you get at communicating, you'll still get into it once in a while, but with the right tools, you can argue less and cause less damage when you do.

Do you really enjoy those
I-told-you-so moments?

Do you keep score of who does what
around your house?

Ever find yourself waiting for a
chance to pay back your husband for
some slight or insult?

Give up the tit for tat.

It's Saturday morning, and I'd love to sleep in, but the alarm goes off at 6:00 a.m., and I climb out of bed and hurry to grab a shower before the babies wake up. Before I can even get the water running, one or both of our infant twins starts to whine and cry. No time for luxuriating in the bath, I throw on some clothes and grab my son to get him fed, and then I switch off to feed my daughter while my son lies next to us. The day's bottles need to be made, so I get that out of the way and then cook breakfast for myself with a spatula in my right hand and one of the babies on my shoulder. Finally, I get the twins bathed and dressed.

Where is my husband during this Saturday morning madness? Still in the bed, since I didn't ask him to get up. Of course, I'm already pissed at him for going out to happy hour last night instead of coming right home from work to help me, so I'm not about to ask him for help now. Instead, I'll show him. I'll find somewhere else to be all day, and he can stay home by himself. I load the two babies in two carriers and head out to Wal-Mart or Target or wherever we can go to kill time and still seem like we're doing something productive. Then it's back home to wash a load of laundry, clean the kitchen, vacuum the floors—all this done while holding one of the twins and listening to the other demand his or her turn.

That stressful scenario happened more than once in the early days after our children were born. I resented how my husband chose to spend his time. I was tired, and I needed help, but he stayed late for meetings at work, went to happy hour with his co-workers, traveled out of town, and played golf on the weekends. Worst of all, when he was at home, he'd lie in bed while I ran around taking care of the housework and the kids. He'd get up if I asked him to, but I wanted him to take that initiative on his own.

What was my solution to our conflict? I decided I could give as good as I got. If he planned a trip out of town, I planned a girls' weekend, so I could leave him home with the babies. If he spent too much time away from home during the week or spent a Saturday golfing, I made sure I spent the next Saturday out of the house. If I didn't have anything I needed to do, I'd create something. I got my hair done, my toes done, went to a friend's house, walked around the mall. Even though a part of me knew I didn't want to be away from my little ones all day, I was determined to give him some time taking care of the babies on his own, so he could see how it felt to do it without any help. I was exhausted the whole time, mind you, and would much rather have been stretched out on my couch with my feet up for a few minutes, but I had a point to prove.

Of course, all of my payback didn't change his behavior— except to make it worse. When I left him home with the kids, he handled it. In fact, he did the job better than I did, just to show me he could. And the whole cycle ended up making him want to stay away from home even more. A spiteful attitude and this kind of tit-for-tat behavior played a big part in our divorce.

Here's the truth. My husband and I were both overwhelmed by the extreme left turn our lives took when we came home with not one baby but two. I went from ambitious career woman, driven to succeed at work, still having to meet all the demands of my job and then come home every evening to handle the care and keeping of two tiny, completely dependent human beings. He went from feeling responsible for the two of us to taking on full financial responsibility for a family of four. Even though I was working, in his mind, he had this family to take care of, and it was all on him. Unfortunately, it wasn't until after we divorced that we each began to see the other person's point of view.

You probably don't have a couple of babies screaming in the other room right now. You might not even have children. But maybe you refuse to clean the bathroom because your husband won't pick up his wet towels. Or you don't cook dinner because he forgot to take out the trash. He's going out with the fellas yet again, so you're going on a shoe-shopping spree. He's not reaching out to you, so you're not reaching out to him.

Here's what I know now. Being spiteful leaves you exhausted mentally, spiritually, and physically. You don't have to live with those lingering issues in your house. If you have a problem with your husband, deal with it directly. Send the kids to your girlfriend's house, call your husband in the room, and sit down to talk. And I don't mean sit him down and start accusing him. Humble yourself, swallow your pride, and apologize for your part in the situation. If you're thinking your husband will never participate in that conversation, then you've got bigger problems. A man who respects you will give you the opportunity to address the issue. Deal with what's at the bottom of the whole thing. Turn it around before it's too late.

Ever tried to prove a point
by exposing your husband's
shortcomings to other people?

Do you think it might be satisfying to
bring him down a peg or two?

Do you get frustrated because people
think you're lucky to have him?

Be his
cover.

I wanted to punish him, and I absolutely, positively succeeded.

When we first moved into our house, we were that couple that always had a well-manicured yard. Being from the country, we placed a premium on having a nice yard and on doing the work ourselves. Herman took charge of the work, sometimes raking, and mowing, and planting three or four days a week, but it was also something we could achieve together, as a team. People driving by would often stop to compliment our landscaping, and it felt good.

As our marriage deteriorated, Herman and I not only gave up on each other, we also gave up on taking care of other things, like the yard surrounding our home. I was overwhelmed with the babies, and Herman was swamped at work and weighed down by the new responsibilities of being a father and all that entailed. Day after day, we ignored the yard, and since we lived in a community with a very strict homeowner's association, that was not a smart idea. Our neglect quickly began to show. Week after week, I obsessed over it. Even though things were falling apart behind closed doors, I hated that the state of our yard reflected that truth for everyone to see. I wanted things to look perfect from the outside, even if I couldn't find a way to make them better on the inside.

It got so bad, the home owners association sent notices reminding us we could be fined if we didn't clean up the mess. Talk about embarrassing. Worried about the kind of impression we were creating in the neighborhood, I did what I could on my own. I didn't push a mower, but I raked and went out and bought the mulch I hoped Herman would spread around. Those bags of mulch sat in our garage for five months. I nagged and demanded, but it was clear he wasn't going to get out there and make things the way they used to be. I thought he was doing it to spite me, and at some point, as I kept hounding him, he probably was.

When you walk by him at home, reach out and touch him in a way that lets him know you want him.

There was a particular section in the back of the house that needed real work. Because the hay we usually covered the ground with hadn't been replenished, it was just a patch of dirt back there, and weeds shot up between the shrubs. When I reached my limit, I ordered forty or fifty bales of hay. I was determined the job was going to get done, and I went to Herman with a determination to make him do it. "I'll help you," I said. "I'll get someone to watch the kids for a day, and we can get it all done."

Herman shook his head. "I'll do it myself. Don't worry about it."

I kept pushing, but he wouldn't budge. The issue became a power struggle between us. He knew it was one of those things I couldn't possibly manage by myself, and his way of exerting control was to withhold his help. I wanted him to do the job when and how I wanted it done. Neither one of us could win. Try as I might, I certainly couldn't force him to do anything.

But I wasn't giving up that easily.

One weekend, I called a few of his friends and told them we needed their help. I invited them over for a cook out and asked them to bring their gloves and help with the yard work. Of course, I implied that Herman was on board with my plan, but I sent him to the store, hoping we could get started before he got back.

Now, these men aren't stupid. They're his friends, so they know how he is, and at least one of them—maybe all—knew I was lying. For one thing, Herman took pride in taking care of his own yard. For another, he'd never have his wife call a bunch of men and ask for that kind of help. But they didn't want to be disrespectful to me, so a couple of them came over and got to work.

As soon as Herman returned, he asked what the guys were doing in the yard, and I told him, "They came to help, since you didn't have time to do it."

Never one to bring other people into our marital drama, Herman played along, but his friends could tell something was wrong. They worked in the yard for a few hours, but Herman's usually the one to man the grill, so the food didn't get cooked, and the party atmosphere I thought I could pull off died before it started. The men left, and it was just the two of us, husband and wife, in a quiet house.

"So," I said, "are we going to finish the yard?" I had poked the bear one time too many.

Herman let loose with all the anger, and hurt, and frustration he felt, and the fight that had been a long time coming erupted. Like all arguments, it eventually came to an end, but the damage had been done.

I wanted two things from our yard-cleaning party: to prove to my husband that I'd find a way to get it done without him, if I had to, and to hurt him. I didn't quite pull off the first goal—the yard wasn't completely done—but I certainly succeeded at the second. I stuck a knife in his pride. I sent a message to his friends that said, "My husband can't take care of his responsibilities, so I need some other men to come over and handle our business." Ouch.

From my perspective at the time, Herman was letting me down, and letting down our family and our home, by not helping me around the house. I didn't understand his side of things, and it got to the point that I didn't care. The way I saw it, I'd stepped up my game after the babies were born, and he needed to do the same thing. I was angry all the time because I wanted him to pick up the slack around the house. I chose one of the worst possible ways I could think of to punish him. With a spirit of vindictiveness, I exposed our problems and his flaws to people he cared about.

Later, after our divorce, Herman shared with me how deeply that day had impacted him. My actions diminished him as a husband, as a provider, and as a man. By using other people to make a point in our marriage, I had gone too far, and while he didn't say so at the time, in his heart, he was done with me. It was one of the specific incidents that moved him toward the idea of divorce when the subject came up.

These days, I keep our problems at home, and I protect my husband's pride and dignity like they're my own. Yes, I talk to my girlfriends about minor issues—everyone needs a sounding board sometimes—but I never try to paint Herman as a bad husband or set out to humiliate him. I don't let anyone else put him down either, just like I wouldn't want him running around town bad-mouthing me or standing by while someone tore me down. It's my job as a wife to cover my husband, and I make sure I do it.

It's tempting to believe you can embarrass your husband into changing by exposing his every flaw to the world, especially when you feel like you've tried everything else and nothing works. It's easy to get caught up in seeking revenge or proving you're right by putting him on blast. Don't do it. In trying to rob him of his manhood, you will destroy any trust remaining in your marriage. If he forgets to pay the light bill, or just doesn't have the money, and you have to get ready for work in the dark, the whole world doesn't need to know. Everything doesn't need to get posted on Facebook or spread through your social circle one girlfriend at a time. One of the best ways you can take care of your husband (and yes, it goes both ways) is to take care of his reputation, his dignity, and his standing among your friends, family, and community.

Do you get frustrated whenever he's less than perfect?

Does his small "annoying" habits make you angry?

Do you hold him to a higher standard than you do anyone else—including yourself?

Accept his limitations.

As soon as my husband, a master at making sure everything we needed for road trips somehow fit into the vehicle, fit all the luggage, beach chairs, beach umbrellas, toys, wake boards, and fishing poles into the trunk, the six of us, four adults and two kids, settled into the van. Surrounded by women and children, Herman claimed the driver's seat and prepared to shuttle our family safely to our vacation destination, the way any good provider and protector would. I put on old school music and got ready to listen to our mothers trading back-in-the-day stories. The drive to Florida would take four hours, but everybody was in a good mood and looking forward to getting away from our routine to-dos. Personally, I was looking forward to slipping out for some adult time while the grandmothers took care of the children.

We had planned out the perfect family trip, and it was off to a perfect start, until I noticed the van veering to one side of the highway. Within the first hour on the road, my husband was falling asleep behind the wheel. It was only nine in the morning, so in my opinion, he had no excuse to be tired. Then I remembered he'd gone out with his boys the night before, and the little bit of irritation I already felt started to grow.

With his wife, both of our mothers, and our two kids in the car, I couldn't believe he'd be irresponsible enough to drive, when he clearly hadn't gotten enough rest. After all, as a mom, I would never put my kids at risk like that. After the twins were born, it seemed like Herman constantly nodded off at the wrong times, but falling asleep behind the wheel, that pushed my buttons in a serious way.

Not wanting to start an argument that might upset the children, force our mothers to take sides, and ruin the trip for everyone, I put on a fake smile and offered to drive. I might as well have offered to carry the van on my back because Herman paid me no attention. But as our journey continued, so did his nodding. Every time I suggested he let me take over, he came back with "I'm all right," or "I got this."

Now, let's be clear. I have no problem doing the driving. I'll throw those kids in the car and drive four hours to visit my family, and I don't need a co-pilot along for the ride. I wasn't angry because I might have to get behind the steering wheel, although I'll admit it was more fun to laugh and joke with everybody without having that added responsibility. I was angry because my husband wasn't living up to the superman he was supposed to be. He was falling short, showing he had limits to what he was capable of doing, and I expected more of my hero.

I expected more because he'd always given me more. We met when I was in high school and started dating as he was going off to college, and from the beginning, he took care of me almost the way a father takes care of a child. I was the first in my family to go to college, and when it was time for me to enroll, he helped me fill out my financial aid applications. He wrote papers for me when I needed help. If I mentioned I was going to the mall, he'd give me money, and if he didn't have cash on him, he'd

Never leave
each other
without a
kiss
good-bye.

let me use his credit cards. The Herman I dated didn't allow me to want for anything.

No one had ever tended to my needs and desires like that. This great hero rode in to save me, and I put him on a pedestal for it. I believed this man could move the Earth if I needed him to shove it out of my way. I idolized him, and sometimes I think God had to knock him off the pedestal I placed him on to show me I'd taken it too far.

When my hero became human, I wondered if he was trying to punish me. You see, we got married the first time under an ultimatum—my ultimatum to him, of course. I was ready to be his wife, and I pushed him into it, even though he wanted more time to build his career and save money before we tried to pay for a wedding. Once we'd launched our careers, I decided on my own that the time had come to have a child, and it didn't really matter if he agreed. I knew if I insisted, he would give in to make me happy, and he did. So when he started to show his flaws under the pressures of work and family, I actually imagined it was his way of paying me back for having forced him into this kind of responsibility before he felt ready for it. It didn't occur to me that the man was just human, with his own particular set of imperfections and limitations.

As the pressures of family and career grew heavier and more numerous, he hit his limit in certain areas where I naively believed he had none. Instead of empathizing with what he was going through, I wondered where my hero had gone. I kept pushing him, demanding that he do it all, in the way he used to when we were younger and had fewer obligations. When he responded to my nagging by checking out, sometimes actually falling asleep at the most random times, the way he did on that road trip, I started to question whether or not my husband could handle the pressures of supporting a family. I made up these theories about his behavior, but I never took into account that he doesn't manage stress the way I do. I never considered that he might have a breaking point.

I chose to focus on how my husband's behavior affected me and what I wanted, and my lack of empathy for what he was going through, along with my expectation that he never take off his hero cape, put another crack in the foundation of our marriage. If I had it to do all over again, I would've paid more attention to Herman's limitations before and after we married. I would've adjusted my expectations and treated him like a person, rather than holding him to an impossibly high standard.

Your mate might do his best to show you his strengths and conceal any vulnerability, but you need to pay attention and recognize where he's weak. That doesn't make *him* weak. It doesn't make him less of a man. It just makes him human, like the rest of us. Don't uncover his weaknesses to use them against him or to tear him down. Do it so you can shore him up in those areas. Do it so you can understand how this man, the man you've vowed to love and support, thinks and functions, and so you can respond accordingly. Give your hero room to be human.

Does "head of household" sound like a concept from the Dark Ages to you?

Do you find yourself jockeying for position in your marriage?

Would you rather be single than part your lips to call your husband "the leader" of your family?

Respect your husband's position as head of household.

I'm about to go hard into controversy. Bear with me, please. Just hang in there for a minute. Keep an open mind.

This issue brings up so many emotions—most of them negative-from a lot of women I talk to and have worked with. And it brings up just as much confusion in men. Before you slam this book shut and hurl it across the room, understand that I'm not advocating a return to barefoot and pregnant, women as chattel, or stuffing ourselves into corsets so we can look dainty.

I'm asking you to consider, just for a moment, that husbands and wives have different, well-defined responsibilities and obligations in a marriage.

Let me explain.

Head of household is **not**:
- based on his income
- assigned because the wife earns less than her husband or doesn't work at all
- permission to be dismissive, abusive, or controlling
- a license to make unilateral decisions
- a superior role
- a gender-based division of household or financial responsibilities

Head of household **is**:
- God's desired role for a husband
- a Christian concept and a cultural expectation
- a leadership role
- the foundation of the family
- the ultimate burden-bearer
- the man's duty to care for and protect his wife and children, physically, mentally, emotionally, and spiritually
- a role deserving of respect

I didn't come from a family with this kind of set-up, so in the early years of our first marriage, I struggled with the idea that my husband was to be the head of our household. When I was growing up, my mother ran things in our house. She was the momma and the daddy. She cooked, cleaned, paid the bills, changed tires—if it needed to be done, she did it. And she raised all of her daughters to be independent too. In fact, of the six of us sisters who were blessed to reach adulthood, only two, including me, have ever gotten married. We weren't raised to rely on a man, so thinking of my husband as someone I needed was a stretch. Herman did a lot for me from the time we started dating. He clearly wanted to provide for me and take care of me, but in the back of my mind, I always believed that whatever he wouldn't do for me or give to me I could make happen for myself.

When my husband didn't jump on board with something I wanted to do, I'd look for his ulterior motive. It seemed like he didn't want me to have what I wanted because it would somehow take away from him and his selfish desires. If he had a practical reason for denying me something, it was hard for me to see it. Usually, I'd fight to get my way until I wore him down, or I'd just go out and figure out a way to handle it by myself. I hate to admit it, but I could be a hardheaded, strong-willed bitch, and it landed me in trouble more times than not.

When the twins were still infants, I needed to find a sitter so I could go back to work. I got a recommendation from someone in my church, and because I trusted the church member, I didn't do much to vet the sitter or to make sure she was the right fit for our family. When I came home and told Herman I'd found someone to look after the kids, he immediately said no. The woman lived too far across town, and we didn't know much about her.

But I was the momma, right? The decision was mine to make, and I went to meet her.

She had a nice house and seemed like a decent, caring person. I was concerned about the pit bull strolling around her living room, but she swore up and down the dog would never be allowed near the children. That evening, I came home with her contract, which happened to require our social security numbers.

Herman took one look at the agreement and shook his head. "Do what you want with your social security number," he said, "but don't put mine on that paper."

"She's a nice person!" I said, and I went ahead and hired her. I didn't need his information to complete the contract. I had my own job and income. He had no right to question my judgment, I told myself. But it didn't take long for things with this "nice person" to go bad.

The first red flag: Every time I came to pick up the babies, the dog she swore would never be around them sat right next to them. I don't care how much she loved her dog, I loved my babies more, and I didn't want them to be the victim of any "good dog gone bad" mauling.

The second red flag: One afternoon, I showed up and she motioned for me to get down as I came through the door. I had to crawl across the floor so no one would look through the window and see me. Apparently, she was behind on her furniture payments, and she was ducking the repo man. Whatever was going on with her, there I was, right in the middle of it. A grown woman, crawling around on some stranger's floor, on my hands and knees, hiding from the repo man.

I told myself that none of it justified terminating her services, but in truth, I didn't want to admit I'd misjudged her and put my children in harm's way. I let things go on that way until the day she called to say she planned to move forty-five minutes away and she wanted to continue babysitting Bryce and Asia.

I thought, "That's it!" I left work early and raced to her house to collect my children. She begged me to let her keep them, but it all sounded too suspicious even for me at that point. I got the heck out of there with the twins in tow, put them in day care, and didn't look back.

But the story doesn't end there; I wish it had. A year later, I got a call from American Express. Someone had tried to open a card in my name. Then two more calls came in. The babysitter I'd trusted with our children had attempted to open numerous accounts in my name. When I reported her, the sheriff said they'd been looking for her for a while. Big surprise, right?

You can imagine what Herman had to say. Four words: I told you so.

I deserved it. He'd been right from the beginning, but I was determined that they were "my" babies, I was the momma, and I'd make the decisions just like my momma had for her children. I didn't think he cared the way I did. I didn't understand that whatever his shortcomings, he always had my best interest and the children's best interest at heart. He felt responsible for our well-being, but I saw him as trying to micromanage me and take away my authority, and I wouldn't tolerate it. It didn't occur to me that he felt responsible for the well-being of his family and was doing his best to protect us.

It's not like I learned my lesson from that one situation either. I persisted in my stubbornness and suspicion throughout our first marriage, fighting to run things until the end.

As we matured and worked to build a better, stronger second marriage, I began to grasp how much Herman really loved us. I started to see that he wasn't trying to tell me what to do because he had some hidden agenda. His opinions reflected his love and concern and his desire to take care of us. Even through the divorce, he tried to advise me when he saw me making questionable choices, like purchasing a home I couldn't really afford. Throughout our relationship, he's done his best to protect me—as head of our household, he sees it as his duty—but for so many years I resisted his guidance.

In our second marriage, we make major decisions together. If he doesn't agree with something I want to do, I take the time to listen and really understand his reasons. Rather than treating him with suspicion, I allow him to bring a different perspective to the discussion and give him the benefit of the doubt.

This isn't just about opening up to the possibility that he just might know what he's talking about. I've already addressed that part. This is much deeper. The key is always assuming he's looking out for my best interest. I'll still come back and make my case when I feel strongly about something, but I know we need two "yeses" to move forward with the important things. What affects one of us affects both of us. We're partners. The days of me thinking I'm the head chick in charge are over.

One thing that hasn't changed about me is that I have a tendency to take on a little more than I should, and recently, I found myself overwhelmed. When Herman suggested I should resign from a leadership position in an organization I loved, I didn't want to do it. "It's up to you," he said, after he pointed out how stressed I was and how it was making me impatient with him and the children. He gave me his input, but he ended the conversation with his usual, "Do what you want."

Back in the day, I would've thought perhaps he just wanted me home to wait on him. Or maybe he didn't want me out there widening my social circle. I would've been looking for his ulterior motive. But this time I put aside that kind of thinking and seriously considered his suggestion. His points were valid. It hurt me to let go of my role in the organization—I like to think I can do it all—but it was the best decision for me and for us.

It comes down to this: My husband carries a heavier mental and emotional burden for our family than I do. Yes, I handle much of the day-to-day responsibilities. My list of household chores is longer, especially as his career becomes more demanding, but his obligation is somewhat deeper. When I have a flat tire or end up in a fender bender, when I'm sad or stressed, when my heart is hurting, when the children have needs or are giving me a hard time, or when I want to launch a new project, like this book, he takes it all on. He does everything in his power to ensure it all works out.

Don't get me wrong; I'm his support system too. But my God and our society both place the ultimate burden on men to protect the spiritual, physical, and emotional well-being of the family, and my husband is willing to take on all of that. He's willing to say the buck stops with him. If things fall apart, it's on him.

Talk to your husband about his idea of what it means to be "the man of the house." You may find he's under a lot more pressure than you ever suspected. Take the time to understand what he expects of himself as a husband and how he'd like you to support him.

No matter who makes the most money, changes the diapers, or cooks the meals, a man who takes his role as husband seriously makes it a priority to protect his wife—body, heart, and spirit. It's not an easy job. Any man who does his best to fulfill that responsibility, though he will fall short at times, is deserving of respect.

Have you confided in other men with complaints about your husband?

Do you look forward to seeing some dude, online or in the real world, who makes you smile?

Are you convinced flirting is okay since it could never go further?

Avoid emotional intimacy with other men.

I clicked on my email and scanned my inbox, filled, as usual, with comments on photos I'd recently posted on Facebook. I paged through quickly, responding to each one, until I noticed one message hadn't been left on my public Facebook page. Instead, the sender, the male half of a couple we both knew in passing, had inboxed me.

"You're wearing that dress, girl. I sure hope your husband appreciates you."

At first, I blew it off. If he'd posted something like that on my wall, I would've taken it as a compliment and left a funny reply. And lots of Facebook friends, male and female, message rather than leaving comments. No big deal. We only saw each other socially on a few occasions—and I'd never given him any reason to think we had a personal, one-on-one connection—so

I didn't give it much thought. He couldn't have misinterpreted anything I'd said or done.

I deleted the message, but I live on social media, and I post on Facebook several times every day. This man didn't give up though. He continued to find reasons to inbox me about things I posted—and he wasn't writing to tell me how much he loved his wife. Scandalous!

Of course, I showed his messages to my husband, who laughed and called me naive. Herman reminded me that just because people look like they have a happy marriage or a perfect family situation doesn't mean they actually do. "Men are going to be men," he said, "and they're going to check out an attractive woman, especially a woman who posts a million pictures of herself at her flyest." "Sometimes," he said, "they're going to test you to see if they can take it further than a look and a compliment."

That's exactly what this guy was doing, but because our marriage was in a good place, we joked about it and kept it moving. This all went down well after our re-marriage, and because we'd built a stronger relationship the second time around, the inboxed messages didn't affect us in any real way. However, there was a time when that type of attention could've presented a real threat. There was a time when unexpected attention from the opposite sex could've led to something more. And that attention is never hard to find.

> Send cute or sexy texts to each other in church, at a family function, or while you're watching television with the kids. Sharing the secret adds to the excitement.

Before the divorce, during a time when things had become really strained between my husband and me, I worked in a corporate office. At one point, a particular co-worker of the opposite sex became friendlier and chattier with me—a compliment here, a joke there, offers to buy me lunch. He never took it to the level of obvious flirtation, so I told myself it was okay. As the weeks went on, I started to expect he'd be happy to see me every day, and he clearly was. Enjoying the "harmless" attention, I started taking a little more care styling my hair and choosing my perfume as I got dressed for work. I never thought about it consciously, but I looked forward to our daily chit chat.

Now, don't get me wrong. I felt zero physical attraction to this man. I'm trying to be clear without insulting him, so suffice it to say he wasn't my type in any way, shape, or form. Under other circumstances, I wouldn't have given him a second glance. But Herman and I were arguing all the time, and our home life provided more stress than anything else. Work felt like an escape from the drama, and having someone there who lit up when he saw me and never had a negative thing to say to or about me felt good.

It would've been easy to start a friendship with this man and confide in him about the problems I was having at home, and yes, it was tempting to have a shoulder to cry on when my husband didn't seem to understand me or respond to my emotional needs. I could've found some reason to take this man up on his offers to treat me to lunch. What would be the harm in that? After all, I didn't feel any physical desire for him, and he hadn't said or done anything blatantly inappropriate.

This potential new "friend" made it clear he'd be all too happy to listen to my problems, but like most women, I'm emotional, and sharing my feelings with him would've created a level of intimacy between us. It's impossible to know where that closeness might've led, but I do know it's that type of sharing that opens doors. *Let's meet for lunch. Meet me in the Kroger parking lot, so I can tell you what my husband did this time. Meet me at the hotel bar for drinks.*

I might tell myself it's all innocent, that I just need a friend to talk to, but let's be honest. We all know that if certain men catch you in a vulnerable state, they can talk your panties right off. You might think you'd never let yourself go there, but you could find yourself driving home from the Marriott wondering who you are. You just wanted someone to listen to you, and he was more than happy to lend an ear—and a little bit of everything else.

If I had leaned on that co-worker, or any other man, while I struggled with the troubles in my marriage, it could've snowballed into a moment of adultery or a full-blown affair. In hindsight, I don't think I would've let it go there, but I'm human, and if I had crossed that line, there's a good chance I would've lost my husband permanently. I can't imagine that he would've given me another chance if he found out I cheated. That's a lot to ask of anyone, but for a man with a certain kind of pride, it may have been too much. One moment of feeling desired and heard could've ruined any chance of repairing the marriage I really wanted.

As a woman, you have to realize that taking another man as your confidante can easily evolve into a relationship that crosses the line. I'll be the first to say I don't believe men and women can enjoy that kind of close friendship without the risk of triggering dangerous emotions or sparking bad behavior. Right now, you might be thinking about some guy you consider a good friend, but you should realize that once you enter into a marriage, those kinds of male-female friendships need to have their limits. A deep, close friendship with a man other than your husband can be a dangerous thing. You jeopardize your marriage when you share parts of your heart with another man. That's why you have your momma, your girlfriends, a pastor, or a counselor. If you can't turn to your husband to discuss your problems, turn to one of those people.

It works both ways. It may seem harmless to sit and listen to a man complain about the challenges in his marriage. It may even boost your ego to compare yourself to his wife. After all, to hear him tell it, she's a real witch. Next to a crazy chick like her, you know you look good. You might be the better wife, or he might be misrepresenting her altogether. Either way, that's dangerous territory. You're setting your male friend up to start thinking of you as the better option. Instead, if a male acquaintance or friend approaches you to discuss his marital issues, express a little sympathy, and shut the conversation down. Suggest someone else for him to talk to, and then keep out of it.

Any closeness or confidentiality you share with a man other than your spouse shortchanges your marriage, betrays your husband, and weakens your commitment to what you've vowed to build with the man you chose to marry. It's just not worth the risk, so find your support elsewhere.

Would your house run more smoothly if your husband would just do things your way?

Does it annoy you when he questions your choices or wants to weigh in on your decisions?

Do you always have an "I told you so" ready to fire at him?

Acknowledge that he might actually be right sometimes.

My husband looked up from paying the bills, shook his head at me, and said, "We're under water."

It didn't make sense. He had a great job. We were living the same lifestyle the people around us enjoyed. Why should we be under water? (Notice I assumed none of those "people around us" were facing a similar circumstance.)

Herman explained that we'd been borrowing from our savings to make ends meet every month. We should've been doing well, but paying $14,000 a year in pre-kindergarten tuition had drained our reserves. Add to that all the fees and fundraisers the school tacked on, and don't forget the money we shelled out for the tutors I believed would give our babies the head start they needed. We were tapped out.

I had no idea. Even though my husband had tried to tell me those expenses would bust our budget, I dismissed his input. I knew what I was doing with my children.

We started planning for the twins' education when I was still pregnant with them. A public charter school in our area offered a pre-K option, but most of my friends sent their kids to private school, including preschool, and I didn't want our children to be shortchanged. When the time came for Bryce and Asia to start school, Herman argued that private school was a luxury we couldn't afford, especially since I'd stopped working to focus on caring for the children. He was saying, "No, this isn't the right choice for our family," but I shut him down.

I was too busy quoting statistics and fighting to prove my point. I'd done the research on early childhood education, and I'd talked to other mothers about the fancy educations their children were getting. Herman hadn't done any of that. He wasn't the one taking care of our kids every day. He was just the father, and I wasn't about to leave such an important decision up to him. Our children needed and deserved a private education, and they were going to have it. Shoot. I knew what I was talking about.

I believed with all my heart that I knew best, and I pushed the issue and got exactly what I wanted, until the day Herman said, "I don't know how we're going to make this tuition payment and pay the mortgage this month."

It had to get that serious for me to wake up and realize my husband might actually have been right on this issue. Our children would've been just fine attending the local public pre-kindergarten program. And even if we didn't have a good public option, we couldn't afford what I'd unilaterally decided we could pay.

We were stuck in a contract with the school, and missing mortgage payments wasn't an option, so we tightened our belts and scraped by until the end of the school year. And then those kids went to public school—just like their father had suggested in the beginning.

I have news for you. Ready for this? *You don't know everything.*

Shocking news? Logically, you understand that on any subject there's someone who knows more than you, but as women, we're so accustomed to taking on everything, it's easy to start to think we also know everything. How

The next time you're out with friends, brag about your husband in front of him. Let him hear you telling others how great he is!

quickly we can dismiss our husbands' opinions, especially when it comes to our children or the running of our home, because, after all, he's not doing all that we do.

I don't know about you, but I didn't marry a stupid man. I would have never been attracted to a man who couldn't confidently take care of himself and his family. Yet, I found it easy to dismiss him. I never actually thought he was dumb; I just believed he couldn't possibly know as much as I did on certain subjects.

When you come from an extremely matriarchal household, like the one I grew up in, it's easy to discount your man's opinions and judgments. Our culture values independence, and that value gets exaggerated and distorted when you come from a single mother household or just have a mother, married or not, who ran things. Many girls are raised to believe we can and should be able to do anything a man can do. Even if your parents had a more balanced relationship, you're still inundated by super-woman images in the media. Television and movies and music tell you that women, especially mothers, should know how to do everything for themselves. So why should we rely on our husbands' opinions when they conflict with our own?

Early in our relationship, when I was just a kid and saw Herman as a worldlier, older man, I was all about trusting him to do things for me. He prepared my financial aid papers for college, filed my taxes, gave me money when I needed it, and helped me manage my bills, but the minute his expertise or discernment meant not getting my way, I didn't want to hear it anymore. Even in areas where I knew he had more experience than I did, like buying cars or taking out a mortgage, I resisted the idea that he might be right if his opinion meant I couldn't have what I wanted. And when he crossed into areas that were supposed to be my domain, like raising the kids or running our household, I was quick to push back.

Did I mention that pre-K scenario happened in our second marriage? As determined as I was to build a solid relationship this time around, it was still difficult for me to let go of everything I'd fought so hard to control. That know-it-all attitude led to dire consequences for our marriage and our family, and it was a hard habit to change.

I eventually had to admit that, at times, I'd made a different choice than the one Herman recommended strictly because I wanted what I wanted when I wanted it. I tend to be more influenced by emotion, while my husband is a numbers man who tends to be more analytical and likes to make decisions based on facts. I've had to learn that we provide checks and balances for each other in these areas. My emotion-based decision-making can lead to costly, impulsive choices, and his pragmatism can be short-sighted. That's one of the many reasons we have each other, so we don't go too far to either extreme.

When you and your husband disagree on important decisions, slow down for a minute and listen to his side. You might have more experience with raising children or running a home or whatever it is that you're at odds about, but that doesn't mean he can't have a valid point. His fresh perspective may help you see something you're missing because you're too close to the matter. His experiences are different from yours, but they're no less valuable.

Put yourself in his position. Let's assume he knows more about cars than you do. Don't you still want some say in whether your family's next car is a mini-van, an SUV, or a Smart car? Your opinion counts, and so does his. Give him the respect of considering that he might be right on a subject.

If you truly value your husband as more than a paycheck and a warm body next to you in bed, then you've got to acknowledge that he's an intelligent being with ideas of his own. Think of him as an advisor whose job is sometimes to challenge your thinking and help you make better decisions.

How would your husband feel if he heard the way you talk to your girlfriends about him?

Do you ever look at a woman with suspicion because she has nothing bad to say about her husband?

Does the mention of something you love about your husband draw resentful stares from your friends?

Stop the man-bashing.

Nurturing comes naturally for many women. We bond by sharing our problems and supporting each other through them. Unfortunately, that sharing can take an ugly turn when we get stuck in a cycle of complaining, especially when our husbands get caught in the crossfire. During our first marriage, I found myself so wrapped up in bonding with my girlfriends that I'd invent things to complain about just so I could be a apart of the "men suck" conversations. If a friend said her husband raised his hand to her, I'd chime in about how Herman raised his voice to me—not the same at all, but I wanted to participate. I exaggerated my problems and shared more than I should have so I could fit in and be one of the girls.

At the time I frequently hung out with an amazing group of women. We got together regularly for girls night outs, cookouts and any other reasons we could think of as an excuse to get together. However during our Soirees, we would discuss our marriages and family life. The more we got together and hung out, and the more comfortable with became with one another, the more our get togethers ended with a little harmless man bashing session. I remember leaving some of those conversations sort of overflowing with negativity.

When I got home, still hopped up on all the bitterness from our session, I tried to discuss with Herman some of the issues I'd talked about with the girls, almost looking to incite an argument with my husband. When he didn't bite, I insinuated that he was being defensive and didn't care about our relationship enough to have a serious discussion about it. My accusations inevitably pushed us into nice little arguments that usually had nothing to do with us. I wish I could say I woke up one day and realized this was an unfair characterization of our husbands and I stopped participating in these sessions, but the truth is it took me a little while to put the brakes on my man-bashing. It wasn't that I didn't recognize how damaging it was. In fact, I'd wake up the morning after one of those get-togethers with a heavy cloud of regret hanging over me. Did I share too much? Did I paint him in a worse light than he deserves? How would he feel if he knew what I said about him, true or not? How would I feel if he talked about me like that?

After our divorce and remarriage, I knew it was wrong to run down my husband, but when I resisted joining those same old how-bad-is-your-husband discussions, I noticed a distance growing slowly between myself and some of the women. If I tried to offer solutions or interject with something positive, I caught looks that clearly said, "Oh, so you think you're perfect?" Time and again, I allowed myself to be drawn in. It was just easier than trying to fight the prevailing habit of the group. Part of me thought this was just what women did, and part of me blamed the men. After all, we wouldn't have anything to bitch and moan about if they did what they were supposed to do.

Ask his opinion on important topics, especially in areas you usually handle on your own. Let him know you value his input.

One day, a friend from the group asked if any of us ever felt like there was something wrong with the way we talked about our husbands behind their backs. It was the first time I realized I wasn't the only one who sometimes wished she could unsay some of the mean things she'd said about her man. We all agreed we were blessed to lead the lives we led—lives we wouldn't have without our husbands— and we were diminishing those blessings in the way we talked about our husbands and our marriages.

We decided to institute a no-man-bashing rule in the group at large and shifted our focus to celebrating the good in our marriages. We created couples date nights, that gave us a chance to come together to enjoy each other as married couples. Don't get me wrong, there was still a space to vent about your husband leaving his shoes in the middle of the living room floor, but we cut out the competition to see who could tell the worst story about her husband. We made room in our conversations to brag a little about what we loved about our men.

Of course, not every group of women I associate with is at the same place when it comes to talking about men. In some cases, their problems are legitimate, and they don't know where else to turn. In other instances, they're just comfortable with the practice of husband-bashing, like I used to be. It feels like a topic most women can unite around. Either way, I find the best solution is to stay neutral, meet the woman where she is, and offer something positive when I can. I'm not in a position to correct another woman or tell her what she should or shouldn't say about her marriage. I just choose not to contribute to a destructive way of thinking and speaking.

In our second marriage, I've become more careful about what I say and what I contribute to conversations. One day, a woman I'd just met at a party sat down and started venting about how her husband had been unemployed for way too long. I could see we were headed down a bad path, so I interrupted her with some questions that allowed her to focus on what he'd accom-

Pull your husband aside and pray with him and for him, thanking God for your marriage.

plished in life before his job loss. Her whole demeanor changed as she went to a place of positivity about him. She pulled back her shoulders and spoke about him with a sense of pride. The reality was that she still loved him very much, but she was tired and stressed and worried about their financial future. If I'd gotten on that man-bashing train with her, we could've sat there sipping our wine and tearing down her husband for hours. And I'm sure I would've eventually found something bad to say about Herman.

Wasting hours going in on your husbands with your girl-friends won't help your marriage or theirs. Instead, find a trusted confidante or two to share any serious problems with, always with a focus on solutions, and choose carefully what parts of your marriage you expose. Allow your friends to vent about their husbands when that's what they need, but don't be the one to fuel their anger or contribute your own husband horror stories. Be the one to turn the conversation to the positive, or just be quiet.

Have you tried everything you can think of to fix your marriage?

Are you and your husband both digging in your heels?

Is there still a chance that an objective opinion could help the two of you find some common ground?

Get counseling when you need it, but choose your counselor carefully.

When our marriage ran into trouble, we did what good Christians are told to do. We saw a pastor at our church for counseling. Herman went into it with some doubts, but I just wanted somebody to fix the problem, and I figured a man of God should be able to do it. I did most of the talking, answering the counselor's questions with long detailed answers, while my husband grunted a simple yes or no. He clearly didn't want to be there, but I was determined to make it work.

"April," the pastor said, "I'm not talking to you. I'm talking to him." In hindsight, he was probably trying to win my husband over and get him to engage, but once the conversation turned to how the man is head of the house, I completely shut down. I went on the defensive and explained that if he wanted to be the head, he needed to act like the head. Needless to say, that session didn't do much to improve our relationship.

I believe in addressing issues head on, so I had no problem asking for help. In fact, we worked with a few different counselors over those early years, for everything from premarital counseling to help repairing our marriage after the divorce, and we experienced a huge difference in attitude, philosophy, style, and skill level from one counselor to the next. Herman didn't trust some of them, and others completely turned me off by making me feel like our problems could all be solved if I'd just be quiet and do what I was told. Uhm, no.

Luckily, we found someone who fit our needs as a couple. She shared our faith, but she had also done the academic work of learning to be a counselor. Once she spent a little time with us, she pointed out that each of us had our own issues to work on and offered us the opportunity to see her individually, in addition to coming in as a couple. It turned out to be exactly what we needed, Even though we'd already set the divorce in motion by then and still went through with it, what we learned in her office helped us figure out how to build a better marriage than we'd ever had.

This weekend, have the kids write thank you notes or make cards expressing their love and appreciation for their dad. Don't wait for father's day!

When you turn to a professional for help, you shouldn't be made to feel guilty or like a bad spouse because you get angry at each other, have major screaming matches, or disrespect each other from time to time. Is that behavior ideal? Of course not. But things happen in this world. We don't live in perfection, so any two people in a committed relationship have to deal with all the challenges real life brings. Any so-called counselor who tries to shame one or both of you because of your marital problems is somebody you need to get away from as fast as you can.

You might be resistant to counseling because of cultural biases against any kind of "mental health" assistance, and our society teaches men to see a need for help as a sign of weakness, so many of them just can't think of going there. (Some men, not all!) If you or your husband won't consider counseling, but you haven't been able to overcome some of the challenges in your marriage on your own, you need to ask yourself, and each other, some questions. What do you have to lose? What's the worst that could happen if you seek help from someone sworn to maintain confidentiality? What are you really afraid of?

Maybe you're ready for counseling, but your husband isn't. You just can't convince him that it will make a difference in your marriage. The good news? You can see a counselor alone and work on yourself first. As he watches you put into practice some of the things you learn, your husband may just change his mind and join you.

Whether you choose a psychologist, marriage coach, certified counselor or other professional will depend on your needs. A little online research can help you choose the best option for your situation. No matter which way you go, finding the right person to help you strengthen your marriage can make all the difference.

What to look for in a counselor:

- **A connection with the counselor.** If you don't feel a certain level of comfort in your initial interview (yes, you should interview a few people before you choose one), you need to look elsewhere. How can you reveal your most intimate troubles to someone you can't relax with?

- **A level of comfort between your husband and the counselor.** Yeah, this one ain't all about you. Seriously, if you and your husband have agreed to get counseling, you both have to feel as comfortable as possible talking with this person.

- **A passion for helping couples build a solid marriage.** It should be clear that this person believes in marriage as an institution and is firmly committed to helping you strengthen yours.

- **The heart of a teacher.** Sometimes you just need somebody to tell you what to do. Someone who can give you applicable tips and tools will get results much faster than the person who spends forty-five minutes lecturing you, sits there listening and nodding the whole time, or spews a couple of Bible verses and sends you on your way.

- **Similar values.** A Christian worldview was one of the most important factors in my choice of counselors. Whatever values, religious or otherwise, are important to you, it helps to have a counselor who shares them.

- **Impartiality and respect for both genders.** If the counselor is immediately on one side or the other, has antiquated views about marriage as an institution in which the wife is secondary, or thinks all men are dogs, you're in the wrong place. You need someone who believes both of you have to take responsibility for your marriage and both of you deserve to be treated with respect.

- **Counseling skill.** When we first sought marriage counseling, I was under the mistaken impression that "pastor" equals "counselor." I'm a sold-out Jesus freak. Truly, I am. But one thing I discovered is that everyone called to preach isn't necessarily called to counsel. I ran into too many old school pastors who thought that if I could just be quieter and more appreciative of what my husband did for his family, everything would work out. In the end, I found someone who shared my faith but also had done the work to develop skills as a counselor, had a more modern view of marriage, and could give us more insight than simply saying I needed to submit.

Counseling, coaching, therapy—none of them is a magic bullet for marriage restoration. You and your husband have to be willing to look at your own behavior and the way you interact with each other and make the necessary changes. However, a neutral third party who has your best interest at heart, who believes in marriage, and who brings the right skill set to the table can often help you strengthen your relationship much more quickly than you can on your own. If your marriage is struggling, a little help might be just what you need.

Have the words "That's just how I am" or "You knew who you married" ever come out of your mouth?

Are you really clear on what your husband needs to change, but pretty sure you're fine the way you are?

Do you bristle at the thought of anyone, especially your husband, trying to change you?

Who you've always
been isn't who you
always have to be.

It started as another fabulous party at the Moncrief house. Herman and I were still trying to figure out how to create that happy family we always envisioned, and an important part of that was entertaining. One beautiful, late summer weekend, Herman's family drove down from Alabama to stay with us and enjoy a holiday cookout. As usual, we had more than enough food, and the men handled the grill, while the older women gathered on the deck, and the younger women took over the kitchen.

Around the kitchen table, the conversation quickly turned to our husbands and how we felt about married life. One of my girlfriends made it clear she didn't like her husband hanging out with the guys. She was constantly worried he might cheat, and she didn't trust him to go anywhere without her by his side.

Clearly, I needed to help this sister understand how to handle her man, right? "Ladies," I said, "you have to let men be men. You can't be with him all day and night. If he's gonna cheat, he's gonna cheat." The women acted impressed by my mature, enlightened attitude, and I was impressed with myself for being so levelheaded.

Early in the evening, the men decided to go on an ice run. We still had plenty of ice, but men will be men, right? I was fine with their little unplanned field trip, until the hours started to tick by. My phone didn't ring, and Herman wasn't answering his. Yes, it was Labor Day weekend, and yes, he was also celebrating his birthday, but that didn't mean he could disrespect me by leaving me stuck at home catering to his family and taking care of our babies while he ran all over town doing whatever.

I cleaned up after the cook out, bathed the children, and made sure our guests were settled in for the night. Exhausted from a long day, I fell asleep before Herman returned, but when he and his crew crossed our threshold at three in the morning, I was up, standing at the top of the stairs, ready to let him and everyone else know exactly how I felt.

"I know good and well you're not walking in here at this hour when I've been in this house with your family all day!" So much for mature and enlightened. I cursed him clean out. I didn't care if I woke up every single person in the house. He couldn't get away with abandoning me while I hosted his family and tried to explain away the fact that I didn't know where he was.

My mother-in-law and his aunt tried to calm me down. "Don't do this here," they warned me.

Please. That man knew me, and he should've known he'd come home to one angry wife. I kept right on screaming, but Herman wasn't about to stand there and be berated by me in front of company like that. Instead, he turned around and walked back out the door. Everyone else started packing to leave, and they all headed for home well before the sun came up.

"Fine," I thought. "Let them leave." I was right, and I wasn't backing down. Besides, my husband should've expected me to go off when he got home. He'd known me since I was fifteen years old, and he was well aware of my temper.

Time and time again, Herman asked me to handle my anger differently, especially with him. I couldn't imagine why he would ask me to try to be someone I wasn't. I didn't see anything wrong with how I acted, and because I believed it was an inherent part of me, I didn't see a reason to change. I didn't even consider that it might be better to handle things in a way that worked for him as well as me.

Years after the party incident, my husband and I found ourselves in the middle of another argument. The louder I got the more Herman shut down and refused to participate, but I wouldn't let it go. From my point of view, the only way to resolve things

> If there's someone your husband loves, but you don't exactly share his feelings, keep things cordial by focusing conversations with that person on things you both care about. Most people love to talk about themselves, so spend time talking with that person about his or her interests.

was to keep fighting until somebody won. I followed him around the house trying to provoke him, asking him over and over, "So what you gonna do?" Nothing I said elicited the reaction I wanted, so I kept pushing the issue.

"Deal with it and talk to me!" I screamed. "Be a man!" I told him. Yes, I took it there.

I wanted Herman to engage, and he finally did. "One: you're not talking, you're screaming", he said. "Two: I'm not one of your brothers or sisters. When y'all are done arguing, you're still sister and brother, and you still have to love each other, but you and I don't. Three: This isn't how I communicate, and I don't have to deal with this from you."

Later, my husband explained that he found me completely unattractive when I was screaming and hollering and cursing at him. He tolerated it, but he didn't like it. There was nothing appealing about the image of a woman out of control. I stomped around the house, slamming doors, and throwing things, trying to get his attention when I wanted it and how I wanted it. How could any sane man possibly find that appealing or attractive?

I'd always believed anyone who loved me should accept all of me and not expect me to change, but Herman pointed out that he never loved me for being bratty and hotheaded. He loved me *in spite of* my quick temper and stubbornness. He understood that I was a

> The next time something goes wrong at home, try your best to take care of it before you tell him about it. He'll be impressed and relieved.

product of my environment, and so he tolerated it as much as he could, but it was killing our marriage. Withdrawing was my husband's way of showing me he desperately wanted me to change my bad behavior.

Herman wasn't the only one to call me out for my dysfunctional way of communicating. Years earlier, a co-worker told me, "April, you're a great debater, but if you were a lawyer, I'd beat you every time. You have to learn how to debate the facts and not let it get personal. Instead, you get emotional, you start shouting, you look unprofessional, and because of that, you lose. You lose the argument, you lose the case, you lose credibility."

I dismissed the man completely. For one thing, he didn't really know me or where I came from. For another, I thought I really was a great debater, even if I got my win by shouting down the other person. It worked for me as I was growing up because my family functioned that way. We fought hard; screaming and yelling at each other was pretty commonplace when my family had a disagreement, but by the end of the day, we were always laughing and loving each other again.

Maybe I'd matured by then, but when Herman told me the way I lashed out was a complete turnoff, it finally clicked for me. For the first time, I really got it. I was disappointing and hurting my husband, and for no other reason than it was what came easy to me. Changing the way I handle disagreements took some time and effort, especially when my husband was on the other end of the argument, and I still catch myself going back to old habits at times. But when I fall back on my inherited way of handling things, I no longer expect Herman to just accept it and love me anyway. On our second go around, I've learned to acknowledge I was wrong, apologize, and try a different tactic. I'm willing to change for the sake of having a stronger marriage and a happier husband.

I hear women brag all the time about how they're "keeping it real," and how anyone who loves them knows what they're getting. "That's just who I am," they say, whenever someone points out an area where they may be hurtful, immature, or hard to get along with. The truth is no one comes into the world with a mean, negative, or self-centered spirit. God did not create you or me with a bad temper, a nasty attitude, a smart mouth, or a sense of entitlement. We learn those traits, and if they can be learned, they can be unlearned.

Most of us have a short list of things we think of as deal-breakers in our marriages. We're willing to tolerate just about anything else, even if we're not really happy. Just because your bad behavior isn't a deal-breaker for your husband—at least, not yet—doesn't mean you should stand firm in it, all the while waving your "take me as I am" banner. Do you really want to be a person he has to tolerate? Do you really want to have moments of being ugly in his eyes?

"Well, what about him?" you ask. "What about his bad behavior?"

What about it? We're talking about you right now, and you can only be responsible for your own actions.

The only person you can change is yourself. Turn your focus inward and take a look at the ways you can be a better person. We're all works-in-progress. It doesn't make you less worthy or less valuable; it makes you human. Ask yourself how you can make smarter choices to be a better woman, friend, and wife. Has your husband asked you to change something you thought was a permanent part of your makeup? Is there some behavior you exhibit that might just make you less attractive to him? It could be anything from a disregard for his opinion to an out of control shoe-shopping habit or a need to give a sarcastic response whenever he asks a "dumb" question.

Be honest with yourself about your shortcomings and how they may be harming your marriage. No one's asking you to be perfect, but you know which things really matter to your husband. (If

> Make a real effort to save money on a shopping trip, using coupons or specials. Then show him how much you saved on things you really need. He'll love knowing you care about being a good steward of the family's resources.

you don't know, you need to ask him.) Apologize for the hurtful things you've done. Tell him you're committed to turning over a new leaf. And then do it. Who you've always been isn't who you always have to be.

Do you expect your husband to respond to threats and ultimatums?

How would you react to your husband threatening to leave in order to keep you in check?

Is a short-term victory worth a long-term loss?

Be careful what you ask for.

A man coming home from a long day of work typically appreciates a warm greeting from his wife, maybe a hug and kiss at the door, maybe a chance to put down his briefcase and take off his shoes before family responsibilities fall on his shoulders. That all sounds good, right? But when his wife is unhappy in the marriage, he can usually expect a different kind of welcome home. (Yes, I realize these roles can be reversed, with the man welcoming his wife home after a stressful day at her high-powered job. Gender roles aren't the point here. Stay with me, people.)

When our first marriage started to fall apart, any thought of creating a peaceful home life for my husband went out the window. I wanted him to change, and I figured I could chastise him into doing what I wanted. Even if he was away from home, I'd hit him with nagging text messages and phone calls.

One fateful day, while he was on his way home from work, I texted him to complain about something he had or hadn't done. As he walked in the door, I put down my phone and proceeded to berate him live and in person. Working at my job all day and rushing home to take care of the babies had left me exhausted and impatient, and I wanted Herman to wake up and see how much I needed his help. Of course, we launched into one of our typical arguments. Frustrated and hurt because I couldn't get him to see my point of view and do what I asked, I reached my limit and shouted, "I want a divorce!"

"Fine," Herman told me. "Do what you want to do. You want a divorce, you can have it."

Not the response I expected.

We'd just celebrated the twins' first birthday, and no matter how much we were struggling to make our marriage work, I had no desire to break up our family. To put it plainly, a divorce was the last thing I wanted. Even as my husband agreed that we should end it, I convinced myself that he wasn't serious and that he would apologize and take it back sooner or later. Since I was the one who put divorce on the table, my pride wouldn't allow me to say I wanted to save our marriage. Instead, I waited for him to wake up, see that this fabulous wife of his had one foot out the door, and ask me for another chance. It didn't happen.

> Forget the quick peck as you run out the door in the morning. The next time you kiss your husband goodbye, really kiss him. Less than ten seconds doesn't count!

After a while, I realized that man had no intention of begging me for a reconciliation, so I put aside my pride and admitted I didn't want a divorce. Unfortunately, by the time I tried to work things out, it was too late. My husband shut me down. When he said he was done, he meant it.

It may seem like he reached that point a little too easily, but I'd been throwing "I want a divorce" in his face for a couple of years. As I've mentioned, I unwisely used the threat of divorce to get him to agree it was time to have kids. We'd gone to yet another baby shower, and I'd watched yet another friend preparing to welcome a baby. I didn't want to be an old lady when I had my first child, so I told him "Either we do this, or I'm out." Did I mean it? No. But I believed I could use the threat to bully him into giving me what I wanted.

It seemed to work, though I'm sure that's not the entire reason he agreed to have a baby. He wanted kids eventually, but he gave in at that time to make me happy and to stop the nagging. As the challenges in our marriage grew—both of us working, the stress of caring for the kids, and the lack of communication between the two of us—I started throwing "I want a divorce" around like it was my new mantra. He came home late from work? "I want a divorce." Left his clothes on the floor? "I want a divorce." Looked at me the wrong way. "I want a divorce."

At the bottom of it all, I wanted him to change certain behaviors, mostly to stop staying so late at work and to help me more with the babies. When he seemed not to understand or care about what I was asking for, I resorted to threatening him, as if that would make him change. It may have pushed him to do little things to shut me up in the moment, but the resentment he felt built up over time and finally culminated in his decision to say yes to a divorce.

This was one of the hardest lessons I had to learn: the power of the tongue. You ask, and you shall get. It may not manifest immediately, but if you keep going hard expressing a desire for something, and speaking it into existence, God, or the universe, or the law of attraction—whatever you believe in—will give you what you asked for.

So what can you do when you're ready to let loose with words you'll regret later? Practice a replacement phrase. When you feel like saying "I want a divorce," "I wish you'd just leave," or whatever hurtful thing you might speak out of anger and your own hurt feelings, focus on what you really need or feel. "I need to be alone," "I don't think I'm communicating well," and "I can't talk to you right now," are all a lot safer than throwing around empty threats.

If the argument escalates despite your best attempts to calm things down, or you feel yourself growing more and more irritated, remove yourself from the situation. But don't go somewhere and spend your time thinking about all the reasons your husband is wrong. Get away and change your focus. Spend some time doing and thinking about something else, and come back to the issue with a cool head. If your mouth is moving faster than your brain, and you've already said something you shouldn't have, apologize immediately, and assure him you didn't mean it.

You might get what you want in the short term by browbeating your husband and giving him ultimatums, but imagine the resentment a grown man must feel when you threaten him with punishment like he's a misbehaving child. It can't lead to anything good.

Most importantly, never let the word "divorce" come out of your mouth in anger. You may think he knows you're not serious or that he'd never take you up on a suggestion that you end the relationship once and for all, but don't be too sure about that. Bullying your husband in an effort to get him to pay attention to you or respond to your demands erodes his trust in you and damages the marriage. He may not leave you over it, but it certainly won't make him love you more. Choose a higher level of communication.

Before you jump out of bed at the sound of the alarm, take a moment to get close to him and tell him how much you appreciate him.

Do you say you want a God-led marriage but still think you can solve your problems by yourself?

Are you waiting for God to hurry up and change your husband so your marriage will improve?

Are you worried God doesn't really involve Himself in your life?

Pray.

I leaned over the sleeping figure of my husband, dipped my fingers in the oil, and following the instructions given to me by a minister, proceeded to oil-draw crosses all over our headboard.

Herman startled out of sleep and shouted, "What are you doing?"

He must've had a flash of those "wife murders husband as he sleeps" news reports. He was already stressed out with the pressures of work and our pending divorce, and he'd awakened to find his estranged wife towering over him at his most vulnerable. His family has a running story about how a woman can work voodoo on a man to make him stay with her, so I can only imagine what went through his mind that night. Whatever he suspected, my desperate act only served to further damage the little bit of trust in me he had left.

I'd prayed and fasted, and that bottle of olive oil had to be holy after I finished blessing it. Determined to make God move in our favor, I asked my friends to pray for us. I even called some of Herman's friends and asked them to talk to their friend and pray for the salvation of our marriage. Let's just say their responses varied. It clearly made them uncomfortable that I was pulling them into our messy situation, but I couldn't let that worry me. I had to fix things. I begged Herman to change his mind about getting a divorce, but he was over it.

The more I pushed the worse things got. Nothing was working. My husband wasn't responding to my crying and hollering the way I wanted him to respond, and God wasn't moving the way I wanted Him to move. Nobody can say I give up easily. For six months, I went hard being my control freak, Type-A self. I sought everybody's advice—friends, family, counselors, ministers—and I did my best to implement it all.

The only one I didn't stop to listen to was God. I could feel His response to my non-stop prayers, but I didn't like the answers He was giving me. I acted like I couldn't hear Him say, "Get out of the way, April." It wasn't in my nature to let someone else handle things, not even God. I ignored the fact that prayer is a two-way communication. I was still relying on myself.

I'd answer the altar call at church, take my burdens to the Lord, and turn around and bring them right back home

Give him a Saturday morning wake-up call he won't forget. Use your imagination!

with me. If the Pastor shared a word, I couldn't let Herman receive it on his own. No. I had to force it on him, explain it to him, try to make sure he saw how it applied to him or to us. By the time I finished beating him over the head with it, he didn't even want to hear the message. I continued to pray, but I was also trying to manage things. I had to run into the brick wall of my husband's immovability over and over again before I could get still and listen to what the God I said I wanted to serve had to say about my marriage.

Finally, it hit home. The clouds didn't part with dramatic rays of sunshine pouring over me. There was no talking bush or visits from angels. There were no voices in my head, just a knowing that I was doing the wrong thing. I was asking God to save my marriage, and then I was running out and trying to make it happen in my own way, in my own time—as if God couldn't handle it without my help. Me and my ego had been standing in the way of God doing what I kept pleading for, but I finally reached the point where my faith was strong enough to trust God. I told Him, "I'm done. It's yours. If you don't catch me, I'm just going to fall." It was His will that would be done, not mine.

Things didn't turn around overnight. A lot of damage had been done, and Herman and I went through with the divorce. Once I calmed down and stepped aside, God had room to soften our hearts and open our eyes. We had to do months of self-reflection and honest communication to rebuild our relationship, work that couldn't even begin until I let go. Herman and I both put in tremendous effort, but we credit the restoration of our relationship to answered prayers. We know we couldn't have done it without God working in our lives.

A few years after our second marriage, we moved to another state, so Herman could take advantage of a career opportunity. We were both in agreement that it was the right choice for our family, but when I got there, I felt isolated. I'd left behind a great group of girlfriends, my mothers' group, and all the couples we used to socialize with. My immediate reaction was to pick up the phone and whine and cry to my friends about how I missed everyone and everything back in Atlanta. Sure, I prayed to God to help me make new connections, but at the same time, I continued to pout and complain, and Herman worried I'd grow to resent him for uprooting our family.

I had to check myself. If I really believed God would help me find my place in our new town, I shouldn't have anything to complain about. I dried my eyes and made a decision to stop grumbling about my situation. I had given it to God, and now it was time to walk away and be faithful. I was surprised by how quickly new friends came along once I got out of that negative energy and opened the way for them to arrive.

When I first started writing this book, there were people who warned me not to mention the part God played in saving my marriage. "Readers might be turned off by all that God stuff," they said. I started to doubt my vision for the book. After all, what good is a book nobody buys? As I sat down to write, I tried telling my story without mentioning God, but He kept finding His way back among the pages. The restoration of my marriage was a miracle, and I can't tell the truth without sharing my faith.

I don't have a mission to convert new Christians or try to prove the existence of God. He may use this book to introduce Himself to some folks, but that's between Him and those individuals. My goal is to help each reader have the best marriage they can, avoid many of the mistakes we made, stay out of divorce court, and become the best person they can be.

When your husband says he needs to talk to you, jump on it! Listen, validate his feelings, and don't talk until he's said all he needs to share.

Whatever your faith, religion, or spiritual practice, don't overlook the power of prayer when it comes to your marital issues or problems. Telling God you want to fix your marriage or change your husband isn't the end of the conversation. Pray, be still, and listen for His response. Heed what you know in your heart He's telling you to do, and yes, be willing to give up control when you're called to. You may not always like what you get, but trust that you'll get what you need.

Do you fantasize about starting a new life without your husband?

Does divorce seem like the easy way out?

Are you just plain tired of trying to make it work?

Consider the real costs of divorce.

D ating my husband after our divorce was so different from how we'd left our marriage. When he came to visit the children, we spent time together to see if we could rekindle our relationship, and it was like we were finding our old love again. Since we were also going to counseling, I figured things were on the right track. But one day, my mother pulled me aside to say, "Y'all need to make up your minds about what you want to do." She was concerned that all the back and forth would confuse the children. I wanted the best for my kids, but since they were just toddlers at the time, I didn't think any of it would have a lasting impression on their lives.

The twins were two-and-a-half years old when their father and I got back together. I felt pretty lucky that they'd been so young when we went through the divorce. I told myself they wouldn't remember any of it, that they wouldn't suffer any of the lasting effects of watching their home torn apart. For them, it would be like their family had always been intact. How wrong I was.

After we remarried and the twins and I moved back to Atlanta, we often drove back to Alabama to spend weekends and holidays with our extended families. Most of the time, Bryce, Asia, and I would go up first, and Herman would join us after he finished his work week. On one such trip, the kids and I were driving past the old neighborhood where the three of us had lived in an apartment after the divorce. As we passed a Walmart next to that apartment complex, Bryce looked up from his game long enough to say, "I remember that Walmart."

Asia looked around and added that she remembered the pool at our apartment complex which was right next to the Walmart store, and how her cousin came over to swim. They also remembered how the people in the apartment above us made too much noise, and how Daddy didn't live with us then.

My heart dropped as I listened to my four-year-olds recount the details of life without their father. Don't get me wrong. He came to visit us every weekend, but as young as they were, the children were clear about the fact that he didn't live with us. Like many parents, we'd convinced ourselves that we'd shielded the kids from the worst of what we went through. I was really sure they were too young to have memories of that time. But years later, at eight years old, Asia sometimes still worried that we'd get divorced again. My husband and I may be happily remarried, but we still argue and have disagreements like any other couple, and when we do, we have to make an effort to reassure the kids that it doesn't mean we're breaking up again.

Obviously, many marriages end in divorce, and when they do, most couples won't get back together. I would never advocate staying in a relationship strictly for the sake of the children. If you're constantly fighting and living in a tension-filled house, you're not doing the little ones any favors. I don't know what goes on in anyone else's household, and I don't judge anyone who gets a divorce. How could I? But what I learned after the fact was that I didn't fully understand what the divorce would cost our family. If I had, I may have made different choices.

If divorce sounds like an easy way out, then you don't really understand everything it entails. While the hardest part for me was the effect on the kids, that's just one price we paid. Don't fool yourself into thinking divorce is easy if you don't have children. Everyone who goes through a divorce has to expect to feel the negative effects in a very real way. Clearly, some marriages need to come to an end, but before you put in a call to the divorce attorney running a $499 special on the radio, consider the following costs.

- **The negative impact on the kids.** You don't need a university study to prove to you that divorce can have a negative impact on children. They may lose their sense of stability and worry about being abandoned. Your mental and emotional energy will be taxed to the limit, and even when you continue to show up and go through all the motions, your state, for better or worse, affects theirs. Oftentimes, divorce means selling the family home, leaving the neighborhood they've grown up in, and saying goodbye to friends. That physical uprooting can be painful for them.

Your ex-husband probably won't live the life of a monk just because you're no longer married, so you can expect your kids to have to figure out relationships with his girlfriend, or multiple girlfriends, and down the road, his new wife. We all know successfully blended families, but many families struggle to make things work with his kids and her kids, his rules and her rules, and interference from the exes. And don't expect her to run her household the way you run yours. Her value system won't be a mirror image of yours, and yes, she'll be making decisions for your children when they're in their father's home.

- **Financial losses.** This may be the area people worry about first, but it runs deeper than you may think—even when both people mean well. My husband is that guy who's always going to take care of his family, married or not. From day one, he paid more child support than he was required to pay. Still, I went out and bought a new house and car because I wanted to maintain a lifestyle similar to the one we'd had in our two-income household. The kids were young and wouldn't know the difference, but I'd feel like I cheated them. I didn't want them to give up anything because of their parents' decision to split up.

  Even though the generous financial support Herman gave me couldn't make up the difference between what I was spending and what I earned, it took me a while to accept the fact that some things were now out of reach for me. In most cases, whether the wife already has a job outside of the home or not, both households take a financial hit. It's just basic math. When you split your household income over two separate homes, everyone has to cut back. Lowering your standard of living doesn't feel good. Asking your kids to do it feels even worse.

• **The identity crisis.** As soon as my divorce was final, I went back to my maiden name. I wasn't that woman I'd been when I was his wife, but I also wasn't who I was before we married either. Everywhere I went, I felt like I needed to re-introduce myself to people. It wasn't just that some people still called me Mrs. Moncrief, although that was a part of it. At the core of it, I was also no longer Herman's wife. He was no longer my husband. When people asked about him, I had to explain that we were no longer together, but more importantly, I had to redefine my life without him.

   Don't get me wrong. I always had my own clear, individual identity, but part of how we define ourselves is in relation to those closest to us. Divorce changes much of that, and it takes time and effort to make that transition.

• **An awkward shift in friendships.** Does it seem glamorous to be single again? Looking forward to Friday nights at the club and Saturday night martinis with your girlfriends? Let go of that fantasy. In all likelihood, most of your closest friends are married. It can be tricky to figure out how to shift that friend-ship to new territory when they still socialize as couples and you're on your own. Friendships will start to fade. Some women who never thought of you as a threat before your divorce may worry that you're interested in their husbands, and a few of those husbands may actually see you as ripe for the picking.

No matter how amicable your divorce, some friends will feel like they have to choose between the two of you. Even if they tell themselves you're all still friends, it can be awkward to invite you over for a cookout when your husband and his new girlfriend are already on the guest list.

- **Loss of extended family.** If you've been lucky enough to grow close to your husband's parents, siblings, and extended family, or if he has a great relationship with yours, a divorce can damage or even sever those connections. Sometimes the family feels the need to demonize your ex-spouse to show you support. In other cases, they do their best not to take sides, but it can be difficult, and it only becomes more so when one or the other of you moves on to a new love interest.

- **Part-time parenting.** These days, most fathers expect to have significant time with their children, and they often want 50/50 physical custody of their children. That means any kids you share will spend half of their time not in your home. Yes, it can seem like having a break from the kids would be a blessing, but when it becomes a way of life, whether you want it to be or not, it hurts.

  Take that in, and imagine what it would really feel like to be a part-time parent. Many of the routines and traditions you enjoyed as a family will be changed, diminished, or lost. This is not just about what the kids lose. It's about what divorce takes away from you as a parent.

Don't underestimate the real costs of divorce. It's financially, mentally, and spiritually draining. When your marriage is rocky, it can seem like the life is being sucked out of you. You just want to feel better. You start to think, "Divorce has to be better than this." Maybe it would be, but don't think it will be an easy road. If you make that decision, make it with your eyes open, knowing full well that there's always a price to pay.

Make Saturday mornings bond-in-bed time. Wait for him to wake up, or ask him to wait for you, and use that time to snuggle close and talk with each other without distractions.

Are you under the impression that your husband should know how you feel without being told?

Are some issues in your marriage too touchy to bring up?

Are you hiding your anger and resentment behind a phony smile?

Be solution-driven.

I sat my husband down and told him about my new discovery, a support group for stay-at-home moms. I was so excited about the prospect of joining an association of like-minded women, people who could understand what I was dealing with on a daily basis. All I needed was for him to block his schedule and plan to be home with the kids while I went off to my first meeting.

When I finished my monologue, he leaned back, breathed a sigh of relief, and said, "I'm so glad you finally found something."

I thought I'd hidden how miserable I was over the previous months. Apparently, I was wrong.

Even though we sometimes talked about how difficult it was for me to stay home with the kids twenty-four hours a day, I never came out and told my husband just how bad it was, that something had to change, that after a few months without a job outside of the home, I felt desperate for adult connections and conversations.

Almost as soon as Herman and I remarried, and the kids and I moved back to Atlanta, I started to contemplate where I could work, but Herman suggested I consider staying at home for a while. After all, the two-career arrangement we had the first time around played a big part in our divorce. With me at home, we would avoid the expense of day care for two toddlers, and I'd avoid the pressures of trying to climb the corporate ladder and manage a family and home at the same time. Herman was still in a very demanding job, and though he didn't say it plainly, he needed me to take care of home so he could concentrate on work.

I agreed to try the new arrangement, because frankly, I was tired. I'd done the working single mother thing in Alabama, and it wore me out. As I thought about giving up my professional pursuits, at least temporarily, I envisioned a more peaceful lifestyle. Asia and Bryce would finally get the time and attention I longed for them to have, and I'd make sure our house ran smoothly while Herman focused on providing. It would be a perfect balance for us all.

If you cook, ask him to clean up after, or vice versa. That way neither of you ends the day burned out or resentful.

That beautiful vision turned out to be a pipe dream. For one thing, I'm a type-A kind of mom, and I figured if I was home with the children, I should be teaching them during the day. I set myself up for preschool homeschooling, because I wanted to give them the best possible start. Yes, I was overdoing it a bit, but at the time, I didn't see it that way. I'm also a floor-so-clean-you-can-eat-off-of -it neat freak, so I worked hard to keep everything immaculately clean, on top of running errands and making sure we lived in a well-run home.

I placed the bar so high, no one could expect to reach it, yet somehow I thought I could. I had no examples in my life to follow on this one. The women in my family worked, and most of the friends I made in Atlanta were career women. My mother and my sisters kept reminding me how lucky I was to have the luxury of staying home. But the life of leisure people thought I had quickly began to feel like a prison sentence.

Not wanting to seem ungrateful, I hinted to Herman that it might be good for me to get a job. I even came out and specifically said I wanted to go back to work a few times, but I framed it as part of a routine of complaining about my new circumstances. I couldn't bring myself to engage my husband in a civil, serious, adult conversation about what I needed. Too afraid that it would take us back to the type of bitter arguments that led up to the divorce, I decided to keep the extent of my unhappiness to myself.

Who was I kidding? My stress level affected my mood, and my mood affected my behavior in ways large and small. Herman had seen it all along, and he happily supported me in joining the group of mothers so I could find some of the adult engagement I desperately needed. I made some true friends and discovered a place to share ideas about how to make the role of stay-at-home wife and mother a bit easier.

I ended up staying home with our kids for several years. As I write this book, they're ten years old. I've started a non-profit, and I'm in the process of launching my writing and speaking career, but I haven't gone back to full-time work that would take me away from the family. For now, this is what works for us. The truth of the matter is that I could've tried to find a balance when the kids were younger. I could've had a sitter come in for a few hours a week, or helped my husband figure out some simple ways to help me more, or taken a part-time job when the kids started school.

I never came up with any of those solutions because I never went to Herman and said, "Here's the problem. Let's solve it together." All my hint-dropping and passive-aggressive behavior were focused on the problem without digging in to find a workable solution. Those old habits of burying our issues or addressing problems from a place of anger still come up once in a while, but for the most part, we're much more direct in how we handle any issue that arises.

Recently, a family member faced a financial crisis, and when we stepped in to provide some assistance, Herman suggested it might be good if I got a job so I could help. Even though my focus is on building my own business, and it wasn't what I wanted to do, I welcomed the chance to have an open dialogue about the possibility of me going back to work a nine-to-five to help out. Even though we saw things differently, I remained open to what my husband had to say. And I gave him time to think things through. In the past, I might have gone off, yelling at him and making threats—anything to get him to participate in the discussion on my schedule. This time, I just put the issue out there, and when he was ready to talk about it, we went straight to the solution.

Don't bottle things up or keep them inside in the interest of keeping the peace. Unspoken needs and desires breed resentment, and resentment always finds ways to leak out and eat away at your relationship. When problems or concerns arise in your marriage, approach your husband quickly and openly and from a place of love, but don't keep rehashing what's wrong. Once it's been stated, you don't have to keep going over it. Nine times out of ten, he already gets it. Instead, start to lay out possible solutions and ask for his feedback. Work together to figure out how you can resolve the issue so you both win.

Have you ever wondered why you said, "I do" in the first place?

Are the vows you took with your husband easily forgotten in the face of everyday conflicts and stress?

What exactly are you committed to in your marriage?

Commit, recommit, and commit again.

I'd spend hours in the kitchen, cooking a nice dinner. I don't even like to cook, but Herman was working long days, and I didn't want him to come home starving and find nothing in the house to eat. By the time he was done at the office, I had a nice meal ready and the house smelling good. Everything was perfect, until he walked through the door and said, "Oh, I ordered food at the office."

He'd ordered food at the office. While I was in here slaving away to make sure he wouldn't be disappointed when he got home.

It had happened before, and this time I was so ticked off I stopped cooking for a week. I thought, "If he wants to order takeout, then let him order takeout every day." I didn't want to be stuck in a hot kitchen, doing something I didn't even like to do anyway, especially when he didn't even appreciate my effort.

In hindsight, I can see I was being a brat. Once I stopped to reflect on his intention, I realized he had no desire to hurt me. He was under so much pressure on the job, and he didn't need one more task to do, like calling me to say whether or not I should have a hot meal waiting for him. He needed home to be a place of peace and relaxation.

What did it really cost me, anyway? I had to feed myself and the kids, and if I ended up throwing out a meal once in a while, it wasn't the end of the world. It didn't make sense to sacrifice the state of our relationship at the altar of a little wasted food. I decided it wasn't a battle worth fighting, especially since he had no bad intentions. In fact, his serious intention to provide for our family to the very best of his ability was at the root of his behavior. How could any reasonable person be mad at that?

Making the decision to not allow myself to get angry over something so insignificant was my way of recommitting to the marriage. Of course, our most obvious recommitment happened when we had our second wedding and became husband and wife again, but that was easy compared to the small recommitments we have to make over and over again, every day.

One morning, after his shower, I asked Herman to please remember to put his towels in the hamper after he finished in the bathroom. Needless to say, I went back into the bathroom after he left for work, and his towels were still in the sink. I was livid for about fifteen seconds, but I caught myself. I realized this wasn't nearly important enough to let it ruin my day or his.

In the past, something like that would have set off World War III in our house. Instead of sitting around thinking about it all day and getting angrier and angrier, I picked up the towels and went on about my business. Of course, I mentioned it to him later, but not in an attempt to set off an argument or prove I was right. I merely let him know that I needed him to be more considerate of me. He apologized and that was that.

Every time I feel us sliding back toward a negative place, even in little ways, I reassess and recommit. As a couple, we have to constantly reassess and realign. Every time I decide to make a change for the sake of a better marriage, I'm recommitting to making this thing work.

> Get the electronics out of your bedroom and make it a sacred space reserved to focus on each other. The kids have the rest of the house to enjoy, so feel free to stop them at the door!

In our second marriage, we moved from Atlanta to Tennessee so Herman could take advantage of a career opportunity. Even though my head was on board one-hundred percent, my heart had a rough time leaving behind our friends, the children's school, and the organizations I belonged to. There was so much I loved about Atlanta I wasn't fully ready to give a new town a chance.

Add to that the fact that Herman was working long hours, leaving me responsible for the twins and for managing our home, and leaving me without my partner to talk to about my struggles. It could've been a disaster for our marriage. I did plenty of crying, and the old me, the one from the first marriage, would've blamed him—even though I had agreed to the move.

Instead, I gave myself time to heal. I opened myself up to new people and new experiences. In one sense I was losing it with all the crying, but I managed to be positive through the tears and the pain. I didn't want to add to his stress by acting like the decision we came to together ended up making me unhappy, so I minimized the amount of my sadness that I allowed him to see. Every day, I found a way to tell him how grateful I was for how hard he worked for our family, and I still do that to this day. At the same time, he shows me through his gestures and his attentiveness that he's just as grateful for me and all I do. Every time one of us expresses our appreciation for the other, we're committing again to having a successful second marriage.

How you and your husband demonstrate and strengthen your commitment to each other will depend on your personalities and where you are in your marriage. Regular date nights are a great way to recommit to each other. Put away the cell phone and give your attention to your husband for a couple of hours, and ask him to do the same. And not having a sitter or the funds to go out is no excuse. You can put the kids to bed early and have a stay-at-home date night. The point is to focus on each other, the married couple, not just the mom and dad or the power couple making moves.

> If you go to bed at different times, lean over your husband, place your hand on him, and pray over him while he sleeps. #coveroneanother

Send texts to each other throughout the day. It's such an unobtrusive way to connect. If one of you is busy, you'll respond when you can. The response isn't the point. It's really about what you, the sender, have to say, and how you make your partner feel. You can send sexy texts, to give him something to look forward to when he comes home from work, or you can tell him how grateful you are for some of the things he does for your family. You might think I'm just blowing smoke up my husband's butt when I send him a text telling him how proud of him I am, but there have been many times when he texted back to say, "Thanks. I really needed that." And when he sends me a text in the middle of the day just to see how I'm doing, it means everything to me to know I'm on his mind as he goes through his busy work day.

Slow down and do something just because he enjoys it sometimes. I like to bounce out of the bed and attack the day, but if he has a Saturday morning free and wants to lie there and talk for a while, I slow myself down and stay with him. I could be getting errands and chores checked off my list, but I commit again to my marriage by making the choice to give him something he wants and needs.

We could always rationalize not doing these things because we're both incredibly busy, but that's a big part of how we messed up the first time around. We failed to make our marriage a priority. In our first marriage, I was absolutely 100% committed. But I was committed to the wrong things. I was committed to the fairy tale idea of marriage I'd fallen for as a young bride. No matter how many people tried to tell me that's not what marriage is like, I couldn't hear it. I thought we'd be different. We'd been together ten years, and I was convinced we'd already dealt with any issues that might affect our relationship.

We were so naive, especially me. I thought my determination to live the fairy tale would be enough, but I still left myself an out. If things went really bad, I could always leave. Not so committed, huh?

I didn't know that a marriage is a living, breathing entity. It goes through growth and change, and you have to reinvent yourself and your relationship at each stage. We went from no kids and two careers, to two kids and two careers, to only one career and and now four people to take care of. As all marriages do, our relationship went through many different stages. Throughout those transitions in our relationship, our behavior had to shift in various ways in order to make each phase work.

By sending the texts, cooking his dinner, having our date nights, lying in bed together on Saturday mornings, and just looking out for his wellbeing, I recommit every single day to making our marriage last. There are, of course, circumstances that call for even bigger demonstrations of our commitment to each other—like moving to a new state for his job—and we take those on too. We do it by standing by each other, each of us trying to lessen the other person's burden by remaining positive in tough times and holding each other up when we need it.

Declaring our love and dedication for each other in front of a pastor and our family and friends was a good start, but the real commitment happens on a daily basis. It happens in the little things we do. It happens in the way we're willing to give each other the benefit of the doubt, assume good intentions, and do small things to let each other know we're the most important people in each other's lives.

Would you rather chew glass than lose an argument with your husband?

After a fight, do you like to wait and see if he'll apologize first?

Are you afraid he'll reject you if you try to make up?

Use the gift of touch.

She started it, but I was sure going to finish it.

A group of our closest friends sat around the table playing cards, laughing, and talking, just a fun couples' night at a friend's house. Everything was good until my girlfriend launched her attack on religion—my religion, specifically. What she really wanted was to provoke me so we could have a little drama. It was the routine in our social circle, pick a fight with April and watch her go off on somebody.

Everybody waited to see how I would respond this time. At first, I kept quiet, but she wouldn't quit. Saying my God isn't real? How was I supposed to ignore that?

Before the party, I'd made up my mind not to let anybody drag me into a debate. Honestly, I kind of liked providing the entertainment with a lively discussion. No matter how heated it got, I thought it was all good fun. But Herman hated it. While my husband loved that I had the strength of my convictions, he didn't enjoy watching those conversations turn into verbal brawls. He didn't like seeing his wife out of control, yelling, and wagging my finger. It embarrassed him.

So I really wanted to keep my cool, but my friend kept pushing the issue, and I didn't have it in me to just sit there and listen. I gave her exactly what she wanted.

Herman tried to calm me down.

"But you agree with me!" I reminded him.

"Yeah," he said, "but who cares?"

I cared, and I made sure everyone there knew it.

The party wound down, and we said a pleasant goodbye to everyone, but once we were out the door, my husband stopped speaking to me, and I acted like I couldn't understand why. At home, I stomped around, slamming cabinet doors and throwing things, ready to stay ticked off for a few hours or maybe a few days. I hadn't done anything wrong, and I wasn't about to apologize. Herman was being a big baby. "Get over it," I told him.

We fell into our regular rut. For days, I'd keep up my temper tantrums, and he'd stay at work as late as possible, avoiding any chance of reigniting the conflict. "Excuse me," we'd say with cold politeness as we passed each other in the hallway or the kitchen.

I'd cook dinner for myself, while he sat on the couch with nothing to eat. Or

Institute a firm bedtime for younger kids. That way you and your husband can have an hour or two to catch up and reconnect every evening.

maybe I'd leave the house without saying anything, just to see if I could provoke him to call looking for me. "Where the hell are you?" he'd ask, and I'd count a small victory for me.

There was just one problem. I was tired of being mad. I was tired of the bitterness and resentment lasting for days or weeks at a time. Since I grew up in an arguing, fussing, fighting family, I could handle the disagreements. But I despised the aftermath. I hated that it took us so long to recover and get back to loving each other.

I was torn about what to do, but I knew one thing for sure: our way wasn't working. We had to do something different, but I didn't realize I had to change myself first, and so the fight dragged on as usual. This pattern of blowing up and holding grudges played a big part in our divorce.

In our second marriage, the problems of everyday life soon began to chip away at the bliss we felt at having reunited our family. It wasn't long before we found ourselves in that dark place again. I have no idea how the fight started, but I was throwing things around and slamming doors, and Herman refused to deal with whatever I wanted to argue about. Even after all the pain and the counseling and the lessons learned, we'd started to repeat our old patterns. I stormed off, and he let me go.

With some distance between us, I saw the danger in what we were doing, and in that instant, I decided to humble myself for the sake of my marriage. I needed to take responsibility for the fight—at least for my part in it—and say I was sorry. If we allowed those old habits into our second marriage, we'd end up divorced again, and this time for good. For once, I wanted to be happy more than I wanted to win the argument.

I took a minute to get my emotions under control first. Regardless of my words, any resentment I harbored would be conveyed through my energy, my tone, and my body language. After I calmed down, I approached Herman. It crossed my mind that he might reject me, but I put a hand on his shoulder, and said, "I'm sorry. I'm done with this. Let's move on."

From the look on his face, it was clear that I'd reached him, and physical contact was key to making that connection. A loving touch conveyed a sincerity that words alone couldn't communicate. I had given him exactly what he needed in that moment, a way out of the conflict with his pride intact.

As long as I was pouting and rampaging through the house, my husband felt like he had to be angry too, but as soon as I gave a little—just a little—he grabbed me and hugged me. He didn't apologize the way I had, but I felt his apology in the way he held me and saw it in his eyes. I would've liked to hear the words "I'm sorry," but I chose to let his affection be enough for me.

We're a normal couple, and we continued to have arguments after that day, but whenever I remembered to reach out to him and lovingly touch him, I got a similar response. Over time, as he began to trust that I was sincere in wanting to fix things and recover from our disagreements more quickly, he also started to apologize and take responsibility.

It took him a while to really believe I was no longer invested in winning at all costs. But I kept at it, and over time, Herman began to appreciate my willingness to be vulnerable. He recognized that our relationship was important enough for me to risk his rejection.

Putting aside my pride to apologize, even when I believed he caused the argument, was the hardest thing for me to do. In fact, April, the woman writing this book, doesn't have that kind of humility in her. I had to ask God for more of Him and less of me. I had to ask Him to grant me that humility because I knew I bore some of the responsibility whenever we argued. One person can't fight by himself. Even though I might not have instigated it, I could always offer an earnest apology because I played a part in the whole thing. Focusing on fault wastes time and energy.

My apology also has to come without expecting one in return. Herman is non-confrontational by nature. He'd always rather avoid a fight, but once we're in the heat of things, he's not the apology guy, not initially anyway. He won't come running to say how sorry he is. Even though it can be frustrating sometimes, I accept that about him because I know when I open the door with my own apology, he'll walk through it and make himself available to reconcile with me. Touching him when I say I'm sorry is another way of saying I still love him.

The gift of touch can work miracles, but it's not a cure-all. Sometimes a relationship is so damaged or a disagreement so hurtful that no amount of physical contact can fix it. If you no longer trust each other, your husband may assume you're trying to manipulate him. And no, you can't rely on the gift of touch to try to excuse yourself from outrageously bad behavior. If you're seeking forgiveness because you went behind his back and ran the family finances into bankruptcy or because you went out and slept with another man, let me suggest that you keep your hands to yourself.

In most cases though, touching your husband, while holding love for him in your heart and releasing any resentment you've felt toward him, can transform your relationship. If your arguments have gotten vicious, if the negative consequences—a house filled with animosity, children walking on eggshells, the two of you ignoring each other—are lasting longer and longer, consider using the gift of touch to repair the rift.

When you see a conversation between the two of you headed for a fight, remove yourself from the situation. Ask God to give you peace, discernment, and humility. Stay quiet until you feel calm, not just on the surface but deep in your spirit. Only then should you seek out your husband. Place your hand on his shoulder, give him a hug, or kiss him dead on the lips—whatever contact feels comfortable at the moment—and apologize. Tell him you want to make your home a place of peace and joy, and whatever you've disagreed about can be discussed at a later time when some of the emotion has settled.

Don't be discouraged if he doesn't immediately react the way you want. You can only influence him, not control him, and the response you get will depend on several factors. Consider how bad the argument was, the state of your relationship, and your husband's personality. No matter what, stay in your space of humility and love. If the two of you still care about each other and both value the marriage, he'll eventually become more receptive. This is new for him, and it may take him some time to realize your only desire is for a return to closeness. He may even be suspicious of your motives, but when you consistently put aside anger and ego and demonstrate that your relationship is more important than winning an argument, the gift of touch can be just what you need to reconnect and heal your marriage.

Do the ups and downs of marriage make you feel like giving up?

Is it starting to seem like a mediocre marriage is the norm?

Are you waiting for your husband to read a book and get a clue?

Or are you finally ready for something . . . more?

So now what?

*E*veryting here presupposes there's still some love between you and your husband and at least one of you is ready and willing to work on the relationship. Reading this book won't fix the problems in your marriage. You have to take action on what you've read. You have to be willing to make a change, even when it's difficult, even when you feel like it's not fair that it's all so one-sided, even when it seems like he doesn't care as much as you do.

"How Do I Know When It's Over?"

If your husband is putting his hands on you or kicking your butt, you need to get out of there and get some help. From what I've seen, *almost* anything else can be fixed, but only you know what your real deal-breakers are. For instance, I hear a lot of women say, "Oh, if he cheats, I'm out." But I've watched some of those same people go through adultery in their marriages and recover and rebuild a stronger relationship. For some people, it's an issue they can overcome. No one can tell you where the line is for you. You might not know yourself until you get to that point.

"But My Husband Won't Change!"

Here's a little secret I discovered as I lived through the restoration of our marriage. *It's not about him.*

No matter how hard you try, you can never change another person. However, you can inspire him to change himself by letting him see you're willing to start with your own transformation. At first, my husband wasn't convinced I wanted to argue less, control my temper, and treat him with more respect. He had every right to be suspicious. He'd spent years with the old me, and he'd been burned too many times in our first marriage. It took time and consistency for him to trust that my changes were real.

Believe me. There was a lot I wanted him to change too—a lot! But I'd never been successful in telling him what to do or how to be. Instead, I turned the focus on myself and the ways I could be a better wife. Over time, he saw how committed I was to doing whatever it took to have a lasting, loving marriage. And something shifted in him. He no longer had to defend himself. He took down his walls and started to work on being a better husband.

Sit down and pray and ask God what you should take from this book. Be willing to hear His answer and be willing to follow His lead. You don't have to hear a voice from the clouds. It may just feel like an intuition. Everything in this book might not apply to you, but you'll know what does.

If your husband really loves you, if he's your friend first and truly desires a happy, fulfilling marriage with you, he'll welcome the new you and want to return the favor. Don't expect him to wake up one day and shout, "Oh, Wow! She's changing!" Your focus should be on yourself, without expectation of how he'll respond. Expect nothing. I can't guarantee you that every man will transform into a better husband because he sees his woman becoming a better wife. But I can promise you that if you take this approach, you'll become a better person.

Marriage Menders

Quick Tips to Heal, Restore, & Protect Your Relationship

No matter how much you work on yourself and your marriage, your relationship will still face challenges. That's just the nature of life. One of you loses a job, has a financial setback, suffers the loss of a parent or a good friend, or goes through a midlife crisis. Many of these life events are unforeseeable and unpreventable, but you can choose to let them tear you apart or allow them to bring you closer together. Use the following tips to help you stay on track when the road gets rough.

Stop being a know-it-all.

One of the biggest blessings in being married is that you don't have to know everything! Just like you're the expert on some things, so is your husband. Allow yourself the luxury of having a partner who can help you make decisions.

Worry less about his behavior and more about your own.

Never use your husband's bad behavior as an excuse for your own. Nothing he does can make you mistreat him or abuse the relationship. Take responsibility for your choices.

Treat your husband like a man, not a superhero.

Yes, he's your hero, but he's still a man. Don't place him on a pedestal so high he can never live up to it. Don't expect him to fit some ridiculous image of the perfect man. Recognize his weaknesses, and do your best to support him in those areas.

Make room for the other important people in your husband's life.

Even when you don't instantly click with your husband's sisters, his mother, or that dude who's been his boy since grade school, you have to respect your husband's relationships with the people closest to him. Do what you have to do to find common ground. Don't make your husband feel like he has to choose between you and the other people he cares about.

Never cry on another man's shoulder.

When things get tough in your marriage, turn to God, turn to your pastor, a counselor, your mother, your sister, or your best girlfriend. Never lean on another man. You might not set out to cheat on your husband, but it's all too easy for emotional sharing to become emotional intimacy. Before you know it, you're crying and wondering what kind of woman you've become. Never put yourself in a position your marriage might not be able to come back from.

Decline to participate in negative talk about your husband—or anybody else's.

Whether it's under the pretense of joking or a completely serious bitch session, it's easy to bond with other women over how dumb, incompetent, clueless, or unavailable your men are. But the easy thing to do isn't always the right thing to do. Running your man down like that will eventually affect your attitude at home, make you less patient with his shortcomings, and give you an excuse to be less than the best wife you can be. Find something else to talk about.

If you need counseling, choose carefully.

When you can't figure it out on your own, good counseling can give you the kind of insight the two of you need to get your marriage back on track. But not everyone with PhD after their name or Reverend before it is the right counselor for you. Choose someone whose values align with your own.

Focus on being a better communicator.

When in doubt, shut up and listen.

Don't make idle threats.
Don't play with the idea of divorce, separation, or a "break." Don't threaten to leave or tell him you wish he would get out, unless you mean it. Think seriously about what a breakup would really mean for you and for your family before you part your lips to say you want it. Watch what you speak in to existence.

Put your hands on that man, but only in love.
If your husband is the kind to respond to a loving touch, make sure you offer it to him with the right spirit. Take the time you need to calm down. Release any anger you feel, reach out to him in whatever way he likes, and make sure he knows winning the argument isn't worth damaging your relationship.

Never underestimate how much a divorce will hurt you and the people who love you.
Don't buy into the mythical statistic that says 50% of marriages end in divorce. There are no studies to back it up because it's just not true! As much as the media and your know-it-all brother-in-law might try to convince you otherwise, divorce isn't the norm. While the real statistic is much lower, a satisfying marriage still takes work. It takes a daily commitment to stay together. Yes, a divorce will cost you, but it will also cost the people who love you much more than you can imagine. Sometimes it still has to happen—in instances of physical abuse or when one spouse has no interest in being married any longer—but it's not an easy out. The emotional, financial, and social costs are very real.

Discuss the problem, but focus on the solution.

It's easy to complain and focus on the problems in your relationship. But if you really want positive change in your marriage, you have to constantly look for the solutions. Get to the point. Say what you need to say, and then figure out how the two of you can resolve the issue.

Stand between your husband and the world.

You are his beloved, and he is yours—even when you don't feel like it! When he falls short, don't put him on blast or highlight his flaws for everyone else to see. Focus on the positive in your man, and watch how the positive expands.

Take your burdens to the Lord.

Stop thinking you can figure it all out for yourself. You're not all knowing. Whether your marriage issues are small or large, take time to go to God and ask Him what you should do. Be quiet, listen, and follow His lead.

To change your marriage, start with changing yourself.

We're all flawed, but you don't have to wallow in your imperfections. As you work on becoming a better woman, you give yourself the best chance for a strong marriage.

Be clear on what kind of marriage you want and what kind of marriage God wants you to have.

Whose vision for your marriage are you trying to live out? Don't let television, the movies, or your next door neighbor tell you what your marriage should look like. Shut down all the noise of the world and ask God what vision he holds for your marriage. Anything that conflicts with His word isn't real.

Treat your husband with the respect his position deserves.

It doesn't matter which one of you earns more money. Our society expects a "real man" to take ultimate responsibility for the mental, physical, and spiritual well-being of his wife and his family. If something goes wrong, everybody's looking at him.

That's a lot of pressure. If your husband is doing his best to fulfill his role as head of household, do your best to support him in it.

Respect your role as his wife and act accordingly.

Isn't it a relief to know you're not expected to do everything your husband does? Doesn't it feel good to leave some of the heavy lifting to him?

Let's be real. Being his support system is no easy task, but the beauty of marriage is that you don't have to be doer-of-all-things. You have a partner to lean on.

Renew your commitment to your marriage every day.

Every time you make a decision or take an action that strengthens your marriage, you're recommitting to your husband and the relationship that holds the two of you together. Date night, a loving email or sexy text message, packing his lunch, or encouraging him to take his annual boys' trip—any act, big or small, done with the spirit of love, reinforces your commitment to him.

When you need to refocus on the right things, review the Marriage Menders in this section. Pick one and just do it!

Acknowledgments

The first and most important thank you goes to my husband, Herman Moncrief. Without you, your unwavering love, your deep faith in this marriage, and your insatiable desire to make our relationship work, we would not be here today. This story could never have been written had you not been willing to fight for the marriage you knew we could have, not just for us but also for our children.

Thank you for your help during those long days and nights, when I locked myself away, writing and reading and re-writing and re-reading. You sacrificed home-cooked meals for takeout and helped with the kids whenever you could just so I could get this done, and I am so grateful to have you in my corner. You are the love of my life, "Pondy."

To my children, Bryce and Asia, my greatest inspiration to write this book. You two will never know the impact you both had on this story or how your lives inspired this book. You are the true superstars in this family unit because it was your arrival that forced Mommy and Daddy to deal with the issues in our relationship and to finally consult with God for the help we needed in order to find our way back to one another.

My appreciation for you two goes far beyond what I can share here. Without even knowing it, you helped save our marriage. If it hadn't been for the blessing of two heartbeats, our family would not be what it is today, stronger, more stable, and filled with so much love! You made the difference. I love you, Bryce and Asia! We thank God for you both.

To my writing partner, Candice Davis. You went over and beyond your duties to ensure that this book would be a practical tool for married couples, for those considering marriage, and even for those still in the dating stage. You asked all the right questions and pulled out exactly what was needed to make this book what it should be. Before our work together, I never realized I had it all in me. Your guidance, expertise, and knowledge of writing and of the book publishing business are sheer genius. Thank you, Candice.

To my family and friends who encouraged me from day one with this idea-turned-book, I thank you. It was your compassion and patience in listening to me tell this story of divorce and marriage, over and over again, that pushed me to take a chance and publish our story so that others might benefit from it. I'm grateful to you all for the love and support you showed during the divorce and after.

Within that group of wonderful family and friends who bless me, there are two very important people I need to single out.

The first, my sister Beverly Carroll. You, who love my husband with everything in you and truly treat him like your blood brother, you were the first person who knew all the details of the demise of my marriage, and you never second-guessed my decision to call it quits. You also never questioned my love for my husband, but you respected me enough to allow me to make my own choices.

Somehow, you knew this was a God-ordained journey that we were taking. It was almost as if you could foresee we would one day be telling this story to inspire millions. It was you who I cried to in the middle of the night and who prayed with me and gave me tough love when I needed it. I love you so much, "Beba!" You are an amazing sister. I truly appreciate you being there for me and my family. Thank you, Beverly.

The second, my dear friend Nicole Hurston-Huntley. I will be forever grateful for our friendship. Through it all—the demise of the marriage, my move to another state, and even through the remarriage and my return back home—you never wavered in your support. You always took time to listen, and through the whole process, you continued to check in just to see how the kids and I were doing. Even after I moved away, the distance couldn't weaken our bond.

Most importantly, you never treated me like a failure, even when I felt like one. You have been and still are a great friend, and I'm grateful to have you in my life! Thank you, Nicole.

A Special Acknowledgment

I cannot end this story without thanking the one true God. Without the faith my husband and I shared, even during the divorce, there would be no book, no story of love, loss, and love again. There would be no Herman and April.

God methodically and intentionally orchestrated this story, from beginning to end. No one but Jesus could have brought together a love so genuine and so pure and stepped in to help us rebuild it after we tore it down. The hand of God was working in our lives from the moment we met. Together, we praise and bless your holy and righteous name. You are an awesome God!

About The Author

After a traumatic divorce, April Moncrief and her husband committed to rebuilding their marriage with renewed faith, counseling, love, and prayer. They breathed new life into their relationship by making significant changes in themselves and in the way they interact with and treat each other. With the heart of a teacher, April felt a calling to share what they'd learned with other couples.

As a marriage restoration speaker and workshop facilitator, April Moncrief, known as the "Marriage Maven", gives women and couples practical strategies to build or rebuild a stronger marriage with a foundation that's better able to survive life's inevitable challenges and crises.

A stay-at-home mother of twins, April writes about the joys, challenges, obstacles and triumphs of marriage and family life on her website, AprilTMoncrief.com. April and her husband

Herman, along with their now 10 year old twins, reside in Nashville, Tennessee.

To find out more about April's ongoing journey, or to get more information about her coaching and speaking services, visit AprilTMoncrief.com.

Work With April

Private Coaching

If you've found yourself in that dark and lonely place where divorce looks to be the only option, STOP! Divorce may not be the answer to what's wrong in your marriage. YOU may be the answer.

Are you exhausting yourself trying to figure out how to fix your broken relationship? April can help you:

- Uncover and heal the deeper issues within your marriage or relationship
- Go from constant arguing to loving communication
- Balance family, work, and marriage in a way that works for all three
- Become best friends again

For a **free** consultation to find out more about working with the Marriage Maven, visit AprilTMoncrief.com and click on "Work with Me." Fill out and submit the form. You'll be contacted within 24 hours to set up your free consultation call.

Book the Marriage Maven to Speak at Your Event

Ready to learn marriage success strategies from a marriage expert who lives what she teaches?

Do you want to book a speaker who will be transparent with her audience, someone they can relate to?

How about a speaker that's fun and energetic, one who will bring a sense of humor to the very serious topic of marriage, divorce and relationships?

April Moncrief, the Marriage Maven, has an inspiring story to share with you—one of love, faith, hurt, loss, and ultimately, restoration!

April speaks from real life experience on the topic of marriage, divorce, and restoration based on her own trials and triumphs. She was married, divorced, and then remarried to the same man, all within a span of six years! Through their fourteen years of marriage and remarriage, April has developed specific strategies to help couples strengthen and heal their relationships.

April speaks at women's conferences, church and sorority events, marriage retreats, men's conferences, and more. Her confidence, participatory style of speaking, and ability to relate to common relationship struggles make her an audience favorite.

Visit AprilTMoncrief.com, click on "How to Book April, the Marriage Maven," and submit the form. Someone will contact you within 24 hours.

You're just a click away from booking a dynamic and inspiring speaker for your event!

CPSIA information can be obtained
at www.ICGtesting.com
Printed in the USA
LVOW04s0324051115

461142LV00014B/56/P